PERIOD FLOWERS

PERIOD FLOWERS

*Designs for Today
Inspired by Centuries
of Floral Art*

Jane Newdick

CHARLES LETTS
Letts
FOUNDED 1796

First published in 1991 by
Charles Letts & Co Ltd
Diary House, Borough Road
London SE1 1DW

British Library Cataloguing in Publication Data
Newdick, Jane
   Period Flowers
   1. Flower arrangement
   I. Title
   745.92

   ISBN 1-85238-118-3

'Letts' is a registered trademark of Charles Letts (Scotland) Ltd

Conceived and produced by Breslich & Foss, London

Designer: Nigel Partridge
Editor: Helen Huckle
Original photographs by Jacqui Hurst
Film origination by Fotographics, Princes Risborough
Typeset by Chapterhouse, Formby
Printed and bound in Hong Kong

●◁▷●

ACKNOWLEDGMENTS

In addition to the specially commissioned photographs by Jacqui Hurst,
photographs are reproduced by kind permission of the following:
Boys Syndication 6, 12 (left), 17, 18–19, 20, 21, 22 (top right), 35, 37, 40 (top right),
41, 43, 45 (right), 47, 56, 57, 58, 60, 61, 63 (top left, bottom), 64, 78, 80, 80–81, 83,
88, 89, 90 (bottom left), 90–91, 91 (top right), 92, 101, 104, 106, 107, 108, 109, 111,
115, 122, 130, 131, 134, 135, 137, 138 (both), 139, 142, 143, 144, 147, 151
The Bridgeman Art Library 11 (Bibliothek National, Vienna), 16 (British Library,
London), 27, 29, 31 (Uffizi, Florence), 42 (Christie's, London), 51 (Galleria dell'-
Accademia, Carrara)
Christie's 126
Fine Art Photographic Library 34, 62, 74, 86, 87, 97, 118, 133
J & J Newdick 66, 67, 69, 70
Sothebys 136
The Wallace Collection 93 (by kind permission of the trustees)

The author would like to thank The Weald and Downland Museum, Singleton,
Chichester, West Sussex, and Spriggs Florist, High Street, Petworth, West Sussex
for their help and co-operation.

CONTENTS

INTRODUCTION

❧

Flowers weave their way through our lives in an extraordinary and very personal way from the cradle to the grave and they create a link with previous centuries as few other things do. Their variety and beauty has the power to delight us and at times leave us in awe, while their delicacy combined with strength and tenacity can puzzle or even confound us. We have art and artifacts remaining from the past which remind us how things were, buildings we can use, sculpture to touch and look at, and landscapes we can walk through, but flowers like all plants and animals have a living history which is quite a different experience. The continuity of plants is very special, and only now do we begin to see how fragile it is and how it can break down if habitats and conditions are changed by human interference.

Our garden flowers are relatively safe now that there is a growing awareness of the need to protect and keep in cultivation all the rare and unusual varieties which might easily be lost. There is a small, sweet-scented double wallflower which can only be reproduced from cuttings. Mentioned in Parkinson's *Paradisus* in 1629, it has long been a favourite in cottage gardens and has been kept in cultivation, almost unknowingly, by generations of gardeners. It is available now from many nurseries and its place in history is probably assured, but it is pleasing when one looks at the plant to imagine all those gardeners down through the centuries and to try to imagine their gardens and the other flowers which they grew.

Wild flowers have a special part in history as they have survived without interference wherever man has allowed them to. The tiny white daisies which spangled the lawn last summer are descendants of very similar plants which decorated a medieval flowery mead five hundred years ago. It is a sobering, yet altogether delightful thought. Every period through history has had its important and favourite flowers, changing with the whims of fashion in gardens, houses and even clothes. Flowers have been used as a symbol and icon, as a hidden language or decorative motif and on a totally practical level as medicine and food. For us they are purely decorative and enhance our lives. Now, as always, they have the ability to cheer or soothe, to celebrate or remind in a unique and important way.

Here are pages of history and ideas all based on flowers, inspired by the past but very much part of today. There are arrangements of all kinds, from simple posies to large-scale decorations for special occasions, and all of them make use of flowers which are easy to obtain from a market stall, flower shop or fresh from your garden. In some cases the starting point for an idea has been a painting or image from the past, while other arrangements simply try to evoke the feel of another period through the use of particular colours or flowers. But whatever the starting point, the flowers are the important element. Enjoy them for their colour and style, the way they lift the spirits and fill a room with scent and life, use them more often and grow them if you can.

❧

An intricate box-edged knot garden at Barnsley House in Gloucestershire.

CHAPTER ONE

MONASTERIES
AND
FLOWER MEADOWS
THE MEDIEVAL PERIOD

Medieval England was a country of fields, farms, villages and forests. By the eleventh century there were few parts of the land which had not been travelled through or settled in. Flocks of domesticated animals were kept and crops grown; small settlements grew up where land was fertile and easy to cultivate and where water was plentiful. Threading their way through the whole landscape were flowers. Fields of flowers spread out like a vast colourful woven tapestry through the land from marsh and inhospitable moor to lush river plains and deep forests.

It is hard for us to imagine the variety and quantity of flowers that existed then, now that our truly wild tracts of land remain only in small undisturbed pockets along roadsides, on unploughed upland and in the few meadows left free of artificial fertilizers and herbicides. Wild flowers must have coloured people's lives in an extraordinary way. Flowers, both wild and cultivated, were an immensely important part of everyday life in medieval times – they were used as decoration, food, medicine, for strewing on floors, in drinks, for celebrations and in religious symbolism. Many of these flowers were simply those which grew wild and naturally but there were also foreign introductions and plants which had been selectively bred and improved.

A tiny bunch of flowers picked from the fields and hedgerows suggests the simplicity of a medieval posy.

The Medieval Garden

—◆—

Illustrated manuscripts and books of this time show the medieval garden to be a productive and often beautiful place which served many different functions to the household. Of course many of the illustrations were probably an idealized version of the real thing and they invariably depicted gardens belonging to wealthy and influential people. But glimpses of the ordinary villagers' gardens reveal an order and neatness, a place for everything, and the inclusion of decorative as well as useful plants.

The first and most important element of the garden at this period was enclosure and protection. Wherever people live in groups they have the need to delineate their own land and, in what was still a fairly wild and possibly hostile countryside, enclosure of a safe patch of land was necessary. Even the smallest plot attached to a dwelling would have been contained by stout fencing or walls for those who could afford it. Wooden fencing might have been woven or interlaced or simply made from rows of stakes and sometimes hedge plants such as quickthorn were laid as fencing. Trellising was also used or a pretty edging made from bent loops of pliable whippy branches such as willow or ash.

Within this safe structure could be grown the all-important herbs and a few vegetables as well as scented flowers. There might be a few fowls kept too and possibly bees. Grain and animal fodder crops would be grown outside the gardens in fields away from the house.

While the main reason for a garden must have been the production of food and medicines there seems to be no doubt that the idea of the garden as a place for pleasure and socializing and for interpreting ideas of visual beauty through growing plants took hold during this period. The earliest recorded gardens were those attached to monasteries and religious orders and here there was an obvious link between the garden as a place of spiritual renewal, tranquillity and quiet contemplation and as a means of providing physical nourishment and healing. The image of the garden as an Eden or as an earthly paradise was firmly fixed by the late twelfth century. The secluded, enclosed and safe garden provided the Paradise ideal while Eden, suggesting a wilder, tree-filled, uncultivated garden, was represented in the inclusion of orchards and flowery meads in the larger estates.

Judging by illustrations from this period, gardens seem to have been used for all kinds of socializing. There are numerous pictures of lovers meeting under vine-covered arbours and women walking and talking alongside flower borders. All kinds of games, such as chess, were played outside and people are shown gathering flowers and fruit or making garlands and training climbing plants. The richest households appear to have had droves of labourers to carry out the intensive work needed to keep a large garden in control with only hand tools.

Gardens appear to have been a much used extension to any house and they must have made a wonderful fresh, light and fragrant contrast to cramped, dark and smelly houses. Perhaps the medieval period saw warmer temperatures and dry summers for, judging from illustrations, much of day-to-day life took place outside and grape vines were commonly grown. It seems, however, that many of these vines did not produce grapes and many only gave sour fruit used for verjuice and vinegar, which were used to add a sharper taste to many dishes.

RIGHT *Emilia in her Garden* by the Master of the Hours of the Duke of Burgundy c.1465. It is intriguing to try to identify all the plants growing in this medieval French garden. The garland being made appears to be constructed from petals or blooms sewn tightly together. The white and pink dianthus are probably the materials used for this. Behind Emilia is a scented covering of white and red roses over a finely-made wooden screen – it is definitely more than a common garden fence. A vine flourishes, although the trees are hard to identify. Along the front of the garden runs a little bed containing aquilegia and what might be blue spikes of grape hyacinth, while the small white flowers in the middle could be sweet violets though most have only four petals, and the taller plant beside the aquilegia looks very like a hollyhock.

•◆•

•◡•

LEFT *Rosa gallica officianalis*, the apothecary's rose of medieval times, was used for all manner of scented concoctions. Fresh, the flower has only a slight, subtle smell, but the dried petals have a wonderful lasting rich fragrance. It is also known as the red rose of Provins, brought to Provence from its native Phoenicia in the thirteenth century. Acres of this rose were still grown in France until quite recently to provide petals to make essential oils for the perfume industry.

Apple trees were extensively grown producing mostly sharp, sour fruit for making cider or other drinks. No doubt the early varieties, not far removed from the wild sour crab apples, were better mellowed by fermentation or by the addition of honey and spices to provide fruit for pastes, preserves and sweetmeats. There were also, however, varieties which provided apples both for eating fresh and for drying and preserving for winter food. Pears were almost as important being mostly rather hard-fleshed cooking pears which were made into puddings, jams and pastes or, for those who had no apples, pressed to make perry or pear cider. Nuts were cultivated as well as being collected from the wild and one fruit loved by people of this period and invariably eaten raw was the cherry.

Peas and beans were crucial food which could be stored and these seeds formed the basis of the diet for both rich and poor. Those who could afford it would supplement this starchy diet, which always contained huge quantities of bread and ale alongside the leguminous vegetables, with fish, meat or game. Since peas and beans and sometimes lentils and millet were eaten in quantity, they were often grown as field crops. The kitchen garden near the cottage, on the other hand, would contain the strongly flavoured leafy plants which were used to add zest to the plain diet. Cabbages and varieties of leafy kale would be cooked for hours and made into a sloppy kind of broth. Hot, peppery leaves of the rape plant were commonly used as were turnip tops, and the sharp, acidic flavour of sorrel was appreciated too. Lettuce was cultivated but used mainly for medicines, although the Romans had used it, much as we do, as a raw salad eaten with an oily dressing. Few root vegetables were grown as they were not developed and appreciated until later centuries, but people at this time had a passion for garlic and onions and alliums of all kinds as well as leeks, and these would have formed a major section of the vegetable garden.

Nowadays we tend to classify herbs as plants which are used in cooking and, to a

LEFT Every medieval garden, which had an area of land large enough, contained a small orchard of fruit trees securely contained within stout fencing or walling. Apples were used primarily to make cider and other drinks, and secondly to provide fruit for pastes, preserves and sweetmeats. The orchard was also an important area of the garden for pleasure, particularly in spring when the trees were in blossom and the branches were laden with soft pink blooms.

ABOVE During the summer months drifts of colour would have appeared in the medieval farm garden. Pot marigolds were planted generously and seeded themselves from year to year, and were used in medicines, cheese making and for adding colour and spice to many foods. The blue star-shaped flowers of borage would have attracted bees to the garden and both the leaves and flowers were used in salads and infused in drinks as a stimulant.

lesser extent, in medicines or which are dried for making pot pourris. In medieval times so many of the plants cultivated and collected from the wild were made use of, particularly for healing, that this kind of distinction did not exist. Herbs were often grown in a wonderful jumble alongside vegetables and flowers and every good housewife would know a plant's special properties and be sure to have a ready supply of the most useful herbs, both fresh and dried.

It was in the infirmary gardens of the monasteries that the skills of herbal healing were developed and then maintained long after the beginnings of surgery. The monks studied the effects of certain plants on the human body and compiled herbals listing healing plants and their uses. The normal peasant, unable to read and with no access to such information, relied on quite basic and well-tried remedies passed down from previous generations. Many of the plants that were grown had powerful and drastic properties, but presumably when the only options were a

The medieval garden was first and foremost a place for the production of useful herbs and flowers. Few plants were there by chance or for just their good looks, but there must have been an innate beauty and sense of rightness which came from the functionalism and order of the plantings. This photograph shows a herb garden planted round a medieval house in Suffolk. A carpet of creeping thyme and deep reddish-grey purple sage makes a sea of soft colour in front of the backdrop of the fine timbered building. There is a careful balance to be aimed at in designing a garden around an old building. Using only plants that were available at the time the house was built is limiting and somewhat pretentious, but it is important to keep the spirit of the period alive through choosing older varieties and the simpler species rather than modern hybrids in bright colours and on an unsuitable scale.

LEFT This early fifteenth-century French picture of *Lovers in a Garden* shows a secure medieval garden enclosed within what appears to be strong castle walls. The raised turf-covered blocks which join the walls were built as small seats and often contained scented flowers or herbs such as thyme, which would release their fragrance when crushed. Sometimes the seats were built from stone and then simply filled with soil and sown with grass. Throughout this garden flowers fill the grass and the all-important red and white roses are carefully trained through a trellis fence. A garden such as this would have been a favourite place for trysts and meetings as it was presumably private and contained all the romantic symbols of courtly love.

dubious herbal potion or certain death the medicine had great appeal. Less potent herbal mixtures were regularly taken to ward off imminent illness or to strengthen and protect the body when it was perfectly healthy, and in some cases were used just for the pleasant effect they might have on the senses. Many plants such as borage were able to 'gladden the heart', while others could improve the taste of and add piquancy to dull and stodgy food.

The medieval nose would have been assailed by strong and pungent smells. Hygienic sanitation was unknown and animals and humans often lived close to each other. Houses had smokey smouldering fires lit straight onto earth floors with a small hole in the roof to take away the eye-stinging smoke. In hot weather, food would rapidly have gone rancid and hard-working people, unless very rich, would not have used much water to wash either themselves or their clothes. Cleaning agents were few except for primitive soap, possibly made from animal fat, and sand and earth for scouring. Small wonder that flowers and scented plants were used freely to mask bad smells. Many wild flowers have names which remind us of their use as strewing herbs and air fresheners. The soft, springy hay-scented lady's bedstraw was used to make bedding while sweet violet was used to scent linen and dried to make pot pourri. Rushes, bracken, woodruff and rosemary were among the many different leaves which were gathered and laid on floors, often to a great thickness, to mop up dirt and food scraps and to insulate and provide a certain degree of comfort.

Flowers of the Period

The native bluebell is a flower of copse and woodland edge. It flowers in spring just as the leaf canopy is breaking and it is common under beech, oak and other deciduous trees. In late April and early May, when it is fully in flower, a bluebell wood is a magical place. The scent is powerful but delicious and very like hyacinths which are in the same plant family. The bluebell was not used medicinally in the medieval period, although the bulb did produce a good starch and the juice from the roots could be used to make a type of glue.

The medieval period had its favourite flowers and many of these were chosen for their exceptional fragrance. Scent seems to have had an almost mystical power for people at this time so it is hardly surprising that the rose and lily were two of the most important flowers. They were not the flowers of the humble cottager, who had to be content with wild dog roses from the hedges and the lily of the field or garden anemone, rather than the tall and stately Madonna lily which was grown in prosperous gardens. But there were still hundreds of flowers to cultivate, every bit as beautiful as the rose and lily, and those who could tried hard to create a flower-spangled patch of turf or flowery mead to walk on and sit in.

Spring flowering plants were important for this kind of wild-flower gardening and an enviable plot would have included daisies, violets, periwinkle, primroses, cowslips and gillyflowers amongst the varied grasses, as well as all the naturally wild and overlooked flowers such as clover, speedwell and celandine. Later in the season the flowery mead must have produced ox-eye daisies, which were a great favourite especially for making garlands for church decoration, feast days and celebrations. Daisies were loved for their clean white colour and purity of shape

RIGHT The fields used for animal grazing and hay making would have been studded with flowers, changing with each season. By late summer, on soils which were suitable, golden yellow corn marigold would mingle with scented mayweed to light up the fields in a tapestry of silver and gold.

◦◖◗◦

ABOVE In pastures and meadows, on many different types of soil, the cowslip, *Primula veris*, was once a very common flower. It grew in such quantity that it was gathered to make wine and preserves, which made the most of its sweet honey fragrance combined with a fresh, sharp scent of spring. Flowers were picked to make great balls and bunches and to celebrate the return of spring. Sadly, the cowslip has all but disappeared from the countryside but, allowed to grow undisturbed, it will spread by seed and re-colonize an area of grassland quite quickly.

LEFT Ox-eye daisies are still quite common on poor land and road verges. People in the Middle Ages loved any kind of white daisy flower and this tough, long-stemmed version, also called moon daisy and marguerite, flowered at mid-summer always in great profusion wherever it was happy. It thrives in dry and well-drained soil and, although it could be grown as a border plant, it always looks at its best growing in amongst grass, turning its face to the sun and blowing in the breeze.

•❖•

•❖•

BELOW The pasqueflower, *Anemone pulsatilla*, was once widespread, growing on downland and coming into bloom around Easter time. A dye was made from the plant which produced a good green colour, always much sought after during this period. The flowers themselves, which were quite exotic and special as wild flowers go, were used in posies and decorations for the Easter rituals and feasts. Now extremely rare in the wild, it is grown in gardens in its common purple form or in the red version which is shown here.

and the phrase 'as white as a daisy' was known in this period. Children then, as today, must have strung rows of fragile-stemmed daisies into long chains to wear as a brief decoration and no doubt the petals were used to predict if 'he loves me, he loves me not'. Sadly nowadays the daisy is seen as a pernicious weed and is removed from immaculately mown turf. There is growing interest, however, in creating areas of wild-flower meadows in even quite small gardens so perhaps the daisy will have its day again as we see a return of the flowery mead.

For a flower to be really popular in this period it needed first and foremost to be useful, preferably scented but not necessarily beautiful to look at. For example, lemon balm, or bee balm, insignificant in flower and invasive in character, was much prized for its potent charm for bees in days when the sweetness of honey was highly valued for making sweetmeats and meads.

Lavender, however, was probably the most versatile flower. It was used for scenting and freshening linen just as it is today. Lavender oil has a clean antiseptic and astringent quality which lingers and permeates laundered linen in a delicious way. Imported to Britain from the Mediterranean region, presumably by the Romans, lavender quicky became the household herb *par excellence* once it was found to thrive even in a damp climate if planted on well-drained soil in a sunny position. No doubt the medieval laundress would have discovered that, if she threw sheets and shirts to bleach in the sun spread across a full-grown lavender plant, the sweet scent would find its way into the linen or woollen fibres.

Small pots of lavender were grown to stand in front of windows to sweeten the air in a room and bunches of dried lavender stems were hung in cupboards or on walls to do the same thing during winter months. The flower heads, picked at just the right time, can be removed from the stems and used to fill small bags, although in medieval times they were often simply strewn amongst stored linen. Lavender was also used in various medieval recipes, from syrups and cordials to candied sweetmeats, as well as in savoury dishes along with other pot herbs.

There are dozens of lavender varieties today, some of which have been bred for their decorative qualities rather than for scent. The dwarf, deep purple-flowered kinds are pretty either fresh or dried but lack the intense scent of older types such as the vigorous old English lavender, *Lavendula spica* Grappenhall, which can grow to a bush 3 to 4 feet tall, just right for draping washing over.

Another important medieval flowering plant was the stately iris, grown in many forms from earliest times. The French used the flower as a royal emblem and until the nineteenth century it also appeared in the British Royal Arms. The yellow flag iris, *Iris pseudacorus*, has many homely names from duck's bill to sheep-shears and it must have been commonly found in medieval times along the margins of streams, ponds and rivers. The rhizomes gave a black ink and dye while the rhizomes of the other indigenous iris, *Iris foetidissima*, were used in ale to make an unpleasant sounding purge. Orris root, which provided an important scent fixative, was obtained from the Florence iris, *Iris florentina*. The dried and powdered rhizome smelt of violets and the powder was used as a perfume and linen freshener while the dried roots were burnt to scent a room. This iris is still grown today to produce orris root which is an important ingredient for making proper pot-pourris. The common flag or German iris was brought to Britain probably as early as the ninth century, but whatever variety was chosen every medieval garden would have contained some of these flowers.

A surprisingly useful flower was the small, white, starry-flowered sweet woodruff, *Asperula odorata*. Although its fresh leaves are scentless, the plant contains the substance coumarin, which on drying releases a wonderful scent like new mown hay which also contains coumarin. The whole plant dried was used in great quantities for strewing and scenting linen. The flowers infused make a delicious tisane and were used to flavour wine and water.

The Medieval Interior

Enough buildings from this period survive for us to create a picture of everyday life in the medieval household. Of course the houses which do remain were strongly and soundly built for people of wealth and influence and some of these buildings contain fine carpentry and a good sense of proportion, creating beautiful and harmonious interiors made from the simplest natural materials.

Although we have no direct evidence, it would seem likely that people then, as now, enjoyed having flowers indoors. A walk though a flower-filled meadow must have resulted often in a bunch of picked flowers and although many would have been used immediately for cooking or medicines, a few blooms probably found their way into a jug or jar. Little pots of growing plants were probably stood on a window frame to catch the small amount of light that was available. Windows were kept small in proportion to wall size in pre-glazing days so rooms were quite gloomy unless doors were stood open. Houses were usually simply arranged with perhaps one main room for living and eating in, plus one or two rooms off this for sleeping. Grander houses might have had a large double height central room or hall with smaller storerooms and chambers off to the sides and stairs to bed chambers.

ABOVE Now that seed suppliers offer native flower seeds and a wide range of all the old-fashioned grasses, it is possible to create a flower-rich meadow or patch of grass. Soil testing is necessary to be sure of choosing the right flower varieties and it may take several years to establish anything like this wonderful hay meadow mixture of red clover, buttercups, dandelions, plantains and different grasses.

RIGHT Here, a bunch of brilliant flowers are the only fresh things in a storeroom full of dried herbs and vegetables. The poppies, cornflowers and corn marigolds would have grown abundantly amongst medieval crops, while the pot marigolds and camomile might have been gathered from the herb garden. They are all simple seed-packet flowers which are worth growing every year to pick for pretty arrangements.

•◆•

•◆•

LEFT A posy of common wild flowers and garden weeds may not be sophisticated, but it has a simplicity and brightness which more than compensates for this. Resist picking flowers from the wild and grow more native flowers in your garden, which you can gather with a clear conscience. This small bunch of marsh marigold, cowslip, vetch, dandelion and periwinkle are just the kinds of flowers that grew in the wild in the medieval period and were also brought into the gardens to add colour, or, in some cases, for their healing and herbal properties.

Furniture was very sparse and even the wealthiest houses would have had only benches for seating at a large refectory table and chests or coffers for storage. Standing cupboards were not common until later centuries.

There were really no pieces of furniture that were not used regularly, so flat empty surfaces on which to stand decorations were not available. The dining table would have provided the largest horizontal space but one imagines that this was normally covered with food being prepared or being eaten. There were plenty of containers, however, ranging from pottery jars, bowls and flagons, to leather jugs, wooden bowls and buckets, woven baskets for everyday carrying and storage purposes and in wealthy houses quite fine pieces of glass and ceramic. In medieval

Flowers were made use of in many medieval dishes to add spice and colour to dull and sometimes bland staple ingredients. Tansy, which has a very pungent smell and bitter taste, was used in a kind of pancake eaten at Lent more as a purgative than a pleasure. Fresh and dried pot marigold petals have a slightly spicy taste which made them useful additions to stews and broths. Marigolds also gave cheese a good colour and had a slight curdling effect on milk. The bright and cheerful colours of both flowers must also have meant that they were often picked simply to decorate a room and add a spark of brilliant colour to very colourless surroundings.

The medieval house or farm in late summer and early autumn would have been filled with the scents and colours of fruits, seeds and flowers, gathered ready to make preserves, potions, medicines and sweetmeats to store away for the winter months. Drying was an easy and effective method of preservation, and other methods such as smoking and curing were perfected to be sure of safe supplies to see people through long barren months. Here a basket of green apples and stems of wild plum make a green still life, with twining hop vines and fresh milky cobnuts, en route to the larder and storecupboards.

paintings and manuscript illustrations from Europe there appear to have been very fine and decorative utensils and containers in general use, and the best of these were most likely used to adorn the interiors of churches. There was already a tradition of using flowers in church as a decoration especially on important days in the church calendar.

Only the wealthiest households could afford the pattern and colour that came from embroidery so interiors were usually plain and in all the earth and wood colours inherent in the building materials. People did, however, colour and decorate the walls and often the woodwork in some way. Wet plaster was patterned using combs or other devices which left lines and marks to dry later in a pleasing design. The colour range for paints and washes was limited and patterns might be made from a combination of red ochre and white or black and white. Bold geometric patterns were commonly used but more gentle free-hand designs, based on flowers and natural forms, were often seen. Wool and flax were spun and woven into fabrics for bedding or covers for stone window seats and possibly for simple hangings and draught proofers, but curtains were not common as wooden shutters made more satisfactory protection from the elements.

The few fabrics that were used would often have been left an undyed cream or brown. Some, however, would have been coloured with natural dyes based on plants, roots, bark and fruits. Many of the best and most potent dyes came from fruits such as the blackberry, or the young nuts from the walnut tree which stain almost indelibly if one is careless enough to get the juice on skin or fabric. Many of the flowers which were widely cultivated were also used for making dyes. For example, the flowers of marjoram when mixed with other ingredients produced a deep purple dye which was used for linen cloth. Dyer's greenweed describes exactly what the plant was used for. This wild flower from the genista family was used to produce a yellow dye which, when mixed with the blue of the woad plant, produced the much sought-after green. Later, in the seventeenth century, dyer's greenweed was considered an important enough plant to be taken by the settlers on their hazardous voyage to New England. The colour range would not have been large but the shades and tones within one colour would have been more varied than we see today. Medieval flowers also came in a smaller colour range than now, as there were fewer pinks, oranges and reds.

Church Decoration and Garlands

•◅•

BELOW *Primavera* (The Hour of Spring), by Sandro Botticelli 1445–1510, has a female figure dressed to represent spring with flowers decorating her as symbols of the season. Garlands of flowers would often have been worn around the neck or as a circlet for the hair or to edge a dress or define a waist. In many countries today, important guests have a welcoming garland of flowers placed around them, and in Europe the remains of this custom can be seen in the flowers used to decorate a bride who may wear them in her hair as well as carrying a posy or bouquet.

Garlands of flowers were used often and extravagantly to decorate medieval churches. The Romans had garlanded blossoms into long ropes to be wound and draped around pillars, doorways and arches and this practice continued to some degree into the nineteenth century. Nowadays, flowers are far more commonly arranged into a container or built into elaborate structures for festivities such as weddings and religious occasions. Making a garland would have been slow and fiddly but the result must have been spectacular when church interiors were hung about with swags of red and white flowers.

Despite its short flowering season, one of the most popular flowers for garlands, for religious and secular purposes, was the bright white sweet woodruff. Available from the end of May through early June, it was particularly important as the basis of garlands to decorate churches on St Barnabas Day on 11th June. When processional crosses were decorated with ropes of flowers on feast days, red roses were usually combined with white sweet woodruff to make 'garnishing' as it was known. Smaller garlands, worn by the clergy, were often provided by nurserymen or gardeners who specialized in the trade.

For any feast day connected with Our Lady, the flowers used were white and of

ABOVE There are few medieval paintings which give more than a glimpse into the interior of houses. This detail from the *Adoration of the Shepherds* by Hugo Van der Goes, 1420–1482, shows orange lilies and white iris in a tall decorated ceramic jar and deep blue aquilegia and fringed pinks in a glass tumbler. The floor is scattered with violets.

LEFT The white lily has always been a luxurious and expensive flower and would have adorned only the wealthiest of households or churches during the medieval period. *Lilium candidum*, or the Madonna lily, was widely grown in gardens and is still popular today, but it is rarely seen in flower shops or markets. Instead, a variety such as this *Lilium longiflorum*, which seems to be available all the year round, makes a very good substitute. It has a heavenly scent and the long, waxy, white trumpet flowers last for several days in water. They look best arranged in a very simple, understated fashion, used alone and not cluttered with other flowers or foliage.

LEFT As it dries, woodruff develops the scent of new mown hay, as reflected in many of its alternative names: ladies-in-the-hay, hay-plant, scented hairhoof, sweet-grass and new-mown hay. During this period this small and insignificant-looking plant was used for church garlanding, to strew on floors and stuff mattresses, as a tisane, and to put into wine 'to make a man merrie' according to a medieval herbal.

When fresh, woodruff makes a charming, if somewhat invasive garden plant, best planted in a marginal area or slightly wild part of the garden where it can be free to spread into a white starry carpet. It prefers semi-shade, but is really an easy and undemanding plant which deserves to be more commonly grown.

these the lily was the classic choice when in season. At other times of year foliage such as willow, box or holly was put to use along with many flowers from fields and gardens. Women were expected to spend much time making garlands, but judging from illustrations of the period this pastime seems to have been pleasurable and sociable, usually taking place in the confines of a secluded rose garden and involving a collection of friends and helpers. The Madonna lily, *Lilium candidum*, is still grown extensively in Europe. Most small gardens in rural France have a patch or row of these highly scented lilies for picking to decorate the home or church. It flowers around the time of the feast of the Assumption on 2nd July and it was considered a suitably holy flower to carry the Madonna's name. Probably introduced into Europe from the Holy Land by the Crusaders the lily symbolized purity, and the change from green through to white of each trumpet flower up the length of the stem was considered to have great mystical significance.

The Madonna lily is a fickle and sometimes difficult plant to grow. It relishes the sun on its flowers but likes its roots to be in rich, moist soil. It can be very difficult to establish and, annoyingly, seems invariably to fail if you try too hard to provide the perfect conditions, while a bulb tossed carelessly onto a rubbish heap in a cottage garden may burst into lavish flower. Once established in a place it likes it is long-lived and slowly spreads its coverage. The bulbs should be planted near the soil surface and, unlike many lilies, will tolerate quite limey soil. If *Lilium candidum* is too difficult it could be replaced by the equally highly-scented and trouble-free white lily *Lilium regale*. In medieval times Madonna lilies were grown in rows against walls or fences often with roses alongside as befitted the two most important flowers of the period.

The rose has been in cultivation since the first gardener and has existed as a wild plant in the northern hemisphere since the neolithic age. The early civilizations of Egypt, Babylon, Greece, China and Persia all held the rose in the greatest esteem providing as it did a source of perfume, medicine and aesthetic pleasure. The medieval rose most favoured was the red rose, most likely *Rosa gallica*, which was probably not introduced into England until the thirteenth century although a monk in 1368 wrote that the 'red rose is ye badge of England and hath growne in that countrye for as long as ye mynde of man goeth'. *Rosa gallica* is also known as the apothecary's rose because it was widely grown for its medicinal qualities and for its dried petals which retained their scent longer than other roses.

A famous version of the gallica rose is the *Rosa mundi*, its blooms splashed and blotched with cerise pink, white and red. Although the story that it was named after Rosamund Clifford, Henry II's mistress who died in mysterious circumstances c.1176, is simply a popular myth, courtly love as evoked by the medieval troubadour frequently had a rose garden for its setting. The white rose of medieval England was *Rosa alba*, the white rose of York, and is thought to be a hybrid of the wild dog rose, *Rosa canina*. The red rose of Lancaster and the white rose of York, imposed one on another, became the heraldic Tudor rose which has remained as a symbol for royalty in Britain to the present day.

LEFT This picture of the Annunciation was painted by Simone Martini in 1333. By this time the *Lilium candidum* had come to be known as the Madonna lily and was nearly always included in paintings of the Virgin Mary. The pure white of the lily's petals suggested the purity of the Madonna and as the plant flowered early in the summer, blooms were used to decorate churches on July 2nd for the Celebration of the Visitation of the Blessed Virgin.

CHAPTER TWO

A
TAPESTRY OF FLOWERS
THE RENAISSANCE

The second Tudor monarch, Henry VIII, ascended the throne in 1509 and from his reign through the Elizabethan period until Charles II became king in 1660 there were nearly 150 years of turmoil and discovery. It was a time of flowering – of intellect, craftsmanship, knowledge of the natural world and of the unexplored areas on the globe. A wealth of new plants was found in distant countries and brought to Europe during a golden age of learning about horticulture.

The face of the English landscape changed during this period, but for the nine-tenths of the population who worked hard on the land for very little, life remained much the same as it had been in medieval times. The great forests shrank as timber was greedily felled for building houses and ships and the land was grazed by sheep where the pasture was suitable. London grew from a population of 75,000 in 1500 to one of 200,000 in 1600, with the threat of plague never far away in city or countryside.

Great gardens, such as the one designed and constructed at Hampton Court, retained many of the features of the medieval garden but also showed a change of perspective and an absorbing of influences from other countries, particularly Italy. The architecture of gardens became more elaborate and the plants grown inside them were more exotic and unusual than had ever been imagined. Sir Francis Bacon, writing in 1625, described gardening as:

> 'the purest of human pleasures; it is the greatest refreshment to the spirits of man; without which buildings and palaces are but gross handy-works: and a man shall ever see that, when ages grow to civility and elegancy, men come to build stately sooner than to garden finely; as if gardening were the greater perfection'.

A tussie-mussie of red and pink roses and lavender evokes the colours and scents of the Elizabethan stillroom.

The Flowering Garden

In a map drawn of London in 1560, the rows of houses shown bordering fields around the Tower of London each have their area of land fenced from neighbours, looking for all the world like the suburbs of today with rows of back gardens and houses facing the street. The plots of land, however, are much larger than today's small suburban patch of grass. The average family at this period grew its own basic foodstuffs and sold any surplus at market and even many city dwellers had the means to be self sufficient. There was common land for grazing and fuel for the fetching and always the fruits, flowers and herbs which grew free, wild and abundantly through fields and woods.

BELOW This still life of extravagant blooms by Juan de Arellano, 1614–1676, displays the skills of the early seventeenth-century gardener. This painting, though no doubt done as a set piece or catalogue picture, has a certain naturalness as if the artist simply wanted to record a beautiful bowl of flowers as he saw it in an interior. It is unlikely that this is the case, however, as few gardeners could achieve narcissi in bloom alongside roses and dianthus. The curving glass bowl suggests that by this time containers were being made specially to hold cut flowers in water.

ABOVE This herb garden in Northumbria is based on the idea of a physic garden (see page 41), containing medicinal plants and herbs which were all grown for their useful properties. The cloistered walls give a feeling of calm and monastic surroundings and, although the plants have been laid out to describe their uses, the overall design of the garden is still very decorative and makes a scented spot in which to sit or walk.

Gardeners of this period were skillful and ingenious. They had discovered how to graft and propagate plants and had devised pumps and irrigation systems for keeping plants alive. By the sixteenth century there was a huge variety of some quite specific and useful hand tools, such as grafting and budding knives, invented for some of the very difficult cultivating techniques which were commonly employed. The herb, flower and vegetable gardens were generally looked after by women, as produce from these areas would be used in the kitchens and stillrooms which were a female preserve. Weeding of gardens was also generally done by women until the middle of the eighteenth century.

In a period of relative stability, great houses rather than fortified castles were built and gardens could be constructed with less need for protection, though they were often placed within a moat, and walls, fencing and other barriers were still

used in abundance to give order and control to the space within. One popular feature of the period was the mount, which was an artificial small hill, quite steep, usually made from earth but occasionally from timber and then painted. People have ascribed a sacred origin to mounts but the prosaic interpretation is that they made a good viewpoint to see over high walls or fences to the surrounding countryside. First featured in medieval gardens, by the seventeenth century they were considered to be an essential part of a 'princely garden'. Often at the top of the mount there was a small arbour or sheltered building in which to linger. Single mounts were usually circular but could be square or pyramidal, approached by a spiralling path or steps. Very large gardens might include several mounts and towards the end of their popularity they were often built at the end of a garden. At this same period the passion for elaborate knot gardens was at its height and the mount would have afforded a view over the complete design.

Knot gardens had their origin in the small regular-shaped beds which had been used for centuries for growing plants separately. These beds made cultivation easy, kept plants apart and were an efficient use of space. Many materials had been used to make edgings in order to stop soil falling away from the beds and to prevent plants spreading out of their allotted space. It often made sense to use edgings of living things such as box, santolina or germander which were slow growing and suitable for hard clipping. Slowly over the years very elaborate bed designs developed, far removed from the small squares or rectangles of the old monastic gardens. These areas of complicated pattern became known as knots or knotts and were originally infilled with flowers or sometimes vegetables. Later these beds were built simply for their decorative effect and the infillings became purely visual. Sometimes plain earth or coloured gravels and sand were spread between the little plant edgings, making bright swirling patterns of contrasting colour. The large amounts of clippings taken from knot garden edgings were used to strew household floors over the rushes to keep the air sweet. A collection of knots became known as a parterre. This word was used in France in 1549 but did not arrive in England until 1639 and strictly meant any level area of garden laid out with ornamental flower beds of any shape or size. The knot garden remained a key element in garden design until the new ideas of the eighteenth-century landscape gardeners swept them away.

ABOVE The Martagon lily is a long-lived and beautiful plant which flowers during midsummer, producing stems crowded with elegant spotted blooms. The commonest version is a dusty pinkish mauve in colour, but there is also a rarer, pure white version. It is an unusual lily in that it will flourish on limey soils and can be safely planted in borders and amongst shrubs, or even allowed to naturalize in wildflower meadows or amongst grass. If your plants produce enough stems, they are excellent as a cut flower and will last a long time in water. The Elizabethans loved the shape of the flower heads, which echoed the fanciful shapes they devised for sleeves, breeches and hats.

•◦•

RIGHT The stiff and stately heads of the crown imperial (*Fritillaria imperialis*) have enormous impact in the spring garden. The plant is a native of Persia and Turkey and was brought to England shortly after its arrival in Europe in 1576. The crown imperial is a quite extraordinary and fascinating plant, often mentioned in the literature of the period. In early spring, the bulb sends up the green flower stem and leaves at a tremendous rate. At the base of each flower bell there is always a drop of water, which defies gravity and remains while the flower is in bloom.

Flowers of the Period

•◦•

The Tudor and Stuart period saw the arrival in England of many new plant species. The mechanism of trade was elaborate and worldwide and plants came from the Near East, from all over Europe and, by the seventeenth century, from the New World. Included in the introductions were tulips, which arrived in England in 1578 from Holland. Their popularity was such that during the period between 1634 and 1637 the prices paid for new varieties in Holland reached fantastic heights out of all proportion to their real value. Tulips are forever linked with Holland but were originally discovered and cultivated in Turkey and exported from there, appearing in Vienna in 1554. They were grown and improved by the Turks until at least the end of the eighteenth century, long after the 'tulipomania' in Europe waned.

The tulip of the sixteenth and seventeenth centuries was very different from most of our modern varieties. The petals were feathered and flamed with colour and it was this marking which gave them their fascination. There were three groups of tulip called roses, bybloemens and bizarres. Roses had a white ground

Flowers, fruits and vegetables were always displayed with great care and skill on market stalls, and paintings of this period show the beauty and variety of the produce on offer. In some European outdoor markets today, smallholders sell their fruits and vegetables set out in bunches and baskets, arranged to make it look its best and tempt the public. Even if they have just a handful of beans, a bunch or two of spinach and a few posies of flowers, they present them with great attention to detail and all the artistry of a still life painter. Dianthus, or gillyflowers as they were called, were a very important flower of this period. The spicey scent and flavour of the clove pink were used in wine and ale, and there were many recipes for preserving the flowers to add to salads, preserves and sweetmeats. A sweet pickle of gillyflower petals in vinegar and sugar was made in July, and if it was kept in the dark the petals retained their colour. A few of these bright pink or red petals were mixed into green leafy salads to add a contrast in colour and texture and a sharp but sweet flavour to the bland leaves.

with pink, crimson or scarlet markings. Bybloemens also had a white ground with markings in black, mauve or purple while bizarres had a yellow ground with orange, red, maroon or brown markings. In each case there was a plain flower called a breeder which was simply the background colour. Occasionally a breeder will flower one year with the distinctive feathering or flaking of contrasting colour which it keeps for ever afterwards. This change of marking is produced by a virus infection, a fact not known to the tulip breeders of that period who tried all manner of tricks and devices to encourage the process.

Another bulb which was immensely popular during this period was the daffodil and from the simple wild species breeders produced fanciful new forms, many of

ABOVE In *A Winter's Tale*, Shakespeare gave Perdita the lines: 'The fairest flowers of the season, Are our Carnations and streak'd Gillyflowers.' Many of the oldest pinks and carnations are no longer grown, but there are varieties which are similar to those beloved of the Elizabethans. Dianthus demand very good drainage and light soil in order to thrive and they enjoy a sunny position. They are propagated by slips or cuttings planted into gritty soil during July and August.

LEFT The aquilegia has varieties native to Europe and North America, and was at one time used against liver complaints, although it belongs to the poisonous ranunculus family. It has always been thought of as a cottage garden plant, happy growing in the chaotic conditions of an overcrowded and slightly shady flower border. It seeds itself abundantly and colour crosses occur frequently. Nowadays, there are many bi-coloured hybrids with larger flowers than the simple single colour species based on *Aquilegia vulgaris*. There are both single and double forms, but gardening purists usually prefer the single types. The colour range is large, varying from pure white through pink, mauve and blue to a deep purple.

them doubles. An illustration from John Parkinson's *Paradisus*, published in 1629, shows a plate of narcissus which includes some very elaborate varieties looking more like chrysanthemums than daffodils.

The pale yellow wild primrose *Primula vulgaris* was one of the commonest spring flowers and was probably grown in gardens for medicinal and culinary purposes. Any slight variation in colour or form, however, made a plant a great prize, and from these few plants were bred wonderful oddities – doubles, Jack-in-the-greens, hose-in-hose, jackanapes and galligaskins. These cheerful and friendly names describe the arrangement of flowers on the stem and the formation of the flowers themselves. The Elizabethans tucked these little plants into their knot gardens and cottagers grew a few along paths or under hedges in the slightly damp and shady conditions in which they thrive. The few that have survived through the centuries are those from cottage gardens where the plants received regular dressings of humus and manure which they need to do well. There is a revival of interest in growing the old primroses and polyanthus which are gaining cult status among ardent collectors, but there is nothing like the range of varieties to choose from nowadays that there was in their Tudor and Stuart heyday.

The sky-blue flowers, half hidden in a ruff of filigree green, of love-in-a-mist or *Nigella damascena* were a favourite in gardens of this period and the seeds were crushed and mixed with vinegar to take away freckles on the skin. By the end of the sixteenth century double-flowered forms were grown, but the single variety was seen everywhere, self-sowing itself conveniently from one year to the next. The double form of the peony, *Paeonia officinalis*, was so common during this time as to be almost not worth mentioning, according to John Parkinson, and it is a plant of extraordinary durability. Once settled in, the peony will flower year after year, producing many rich crimson flowers on a large mound of a plant. Sometimes old plants can be found still flowering long after a house and garden are in ruins or have been swept away. Exotic flower imports from as far afield as Peru were *Mirabilis jalapa*, or marvel of Peru, and nasturtium which must have added a flamboyant note to gardens filled with the fairly subtle colours of native English flowers.

The sixteenth and seventeenth centuries saw a developing interest in shrubs and trees as more and more new species were brought into the country. These included the apricot from Turkey, the Judas tree and laburnum from southern Europe and the lilac from eastern Europe. There was a gradual shift from growing mostly native plants as trees and hedges to using imported varieties, although the evergreens such as box, juniper, holly and ivy continued to be important for putting solidity and structure into the design of gardens.

Many new food plants were brought into the country too, including spinach and the first really edible orange carrot from Europe and potatoes from South America. This great influx of new plant material inspired both the writing of the first practical gardening books and the beginning of scientific study of plants in England. In 1621 the Oxford Physic Garden was begun, the first of its kind. Arranged in a very formal layout with rows and rows of plants grown according to species in square beds or complicated knot gardens, it was bounded by high walls and included stately and very grand gateways and buildings.

From detailed accounts of what was spent on plants for the construction of gardens at the royal palace of Hampton Court in the 1530s, it is obvious that by then there were large, professional nurseries providing all manner of plants, some in great quantities. By 1596 John Gerard published a catalogue of the contents of his garden in Holborn in London and listed over 1000 different plants all grown by him. Although he was not a nurseryman, he was a gardener to one of the Queen's great ministers and was obviously a knowledgeable and experienced plantsman, one in a long line from then to the present day.

BELOW This rich crimson, double primrose is a far cry from the simple, pale yellow, hedgerow version found blooming every spring. Many varieties were bred which had elaborate shapes and strange aberrations, with equally extraordinary names. Hose-in-hose types had one flower growing from the centre of another, and Jack-in-the-greens had single flowers backed by a ruff of little green leaf-like frills. These variations on the original simple flower show the Elizabethan love of detail and decoration in their flowers, which was very similar to their taste in clothes – fabrics were often slashed and backed with different colours to produce a striped effect, and stiffened lace and fabric ruffs and frills were worn at neck and wrist. Primroses of all kinds made perfect plants to fill fashionable knot gardens and cottage gardens alike.

Stillroom Flowers

Awoman of this period who lived in a house with a garden large enough to produce all the fruits, vegetables, herbs and flowers required for a household, would have spent much time organizing the work of the stillroom where many of the commodities needed throughout the house or estate would have been produced. There was a seasonal routine to the work as produce had to be gathered, preserved and stored at exactly the right times throughout the year. In quieter periods of the year there would be time to make up potions and medicines from fruits and flowers already preserved. In addition to food items such as jams and jellies, pickled fruits and vegetables, beer and cordials, sweets and comfits, crystallized fruits and flowers, all kinds of day-to-day things were made in the stillroom, including ink and paper, sweet bags or herbs for linen, eau-de-vie, perfumes, candles, polishes, lotions, cold cures, shampoos and toilet waters, rose water, and even bottles of June rain water to use throughout the year.

While stewards in large houses and manors at this time were usually male it was very much a female job to work in the stillroom. Dairy work, brewing and baking and the more hum-drum jobs of cleaning, basic cooking for servants and laundering were overseen by the lady of the house, but she herself would work in

BELOW *Spring* by Lucas van Valkenbosch, 1595, shows the mistress of a grand house and garden who had the important job of producing all the medicines and herbal potions, dried herbs and flowers needed for the whole year. Help would have been necessary to collect the leaves and flowers from the gardens and the countryside, while a whole team of men tended the elaborate plots in an enclosed area designed for growing special plants in separate beds.

ABOVE An informal spring garden has something of the feel of an Elizabethan cottage garden with its cluttered mixture of flowers and shrubs. The double perennial, yellow wallflower, Harpur Crewe, rediscovered early this century, was mentioned in 1696 by Parkinson in his *Paradisus*. This variety is propagated only by cuttings, but has still managed to survive over the centuries in gardens such as this.

the stillroom and write her recipes and cures in a household book which was passed down from generation to generation. She would be expected to know how to do many things from curing a mad dog to making cooling barley water for thirsty hay makers.

The two most important summer flowers in the stillroom were gillyflowers and roses. Gillyflowers or July-flowers were what we now call pinks or carnations (dianthus). They had been grown since medieval times and were highly prized for their delicious clove scent which was put to various uses including adding perfume to sweet bags and flavouring ale and wine. A fourteenth-century variety was called sops-in-wine, and by the Tudor times there were two groups of dianthus, the single type known as pinks and the semi-double kind sometimes known as 'coronations' which came to be called carnations. The single clove or pink gillyflower seems to

LEFT The brief summer period of abundance from the garden means hours spent drying and preserving the harvest. The Elizabethan housewife spent many days working in the stillroom to be sure nothing went to waste. The most important crops were herbs and rose petals, which were dried to preserve them. Fruits were made into jams, syrups and concentrated pastes and stored away for the winter months when there was very little fresh food. Nowadays, we can use produce in just the same ways, but for us the results are a pleasure rather than a necessity, fun to make and good to share.

ABOVE The exquisite rose, Great Maiden's Blush, is the softest pale pink with an informal arrangement of reflexed petals and crisp greyish foliage common to the alba roses. This variety was known prior to the fifteenth century and has been grown in cottage gardens ever since. As the flower opens, the petals slowly fade, leaving the pink blush in the centre of the flower which gave rise to the French name *Cuisse de nymphe*. It makes a large shrub with a slightly untidy shape, but it is a delightful example of an old rose to plant today.

RIGHT All through the summer while roses are in flower, collect petals to dry for pot-pourri and sweet sachets. If you have access to many different rose varieties, dry the separate petal colours singly. When they are fully dry they change colour and are best mixed at this stage into a pot-pourri. Red, pink and some yellow roses retain their colour well, while white blooms tend to dry to deep creams and browns.

BELOW Gather petals on a dry day when the rose has just fully opened. Pull the flower head apart and spread the petals on a proper drying tray, or use a shallow basket, muslin screen, or any flat surface which is perforated to allow the movement of air. Either dry petals quickly outside in hot sun, or put them in a warm airy room to dry more slowly. If it is humid, they may need artificial heat from a hot cupboard or very cool oven. For an old-fashioned moist potpourri, the petals are only dried to a leathery stage before being mixed with coarse salt and pressed down until crumbly and fermented.

have had the stronger perfume of the two kinds. The petals of the gillyflower were dried to make sweet bags along with roses, lavender, and all kinds of herbs and spices. In 1618 William Lawson referred in *The Country Housewife's Garden* to the gillyflower as 'the king of flowers except the rose'.

The most highly used flower at this time was undoubtedly the rose. A recipe of the period required eleven gallons of scented rose petals to make a rose syrup. On very grand estates roses were possibly grown on a large scale like other field crops, and people may have been able to buy large quantities of petals in season from commercial growers. The true oil or attar of roses which is distilled from the petals takes ten thousand pounds of flowers for a single pound of fragrant oil. Most Elizabethan households would have made a quantity of simple rose water and perhaps distilled just a very small amount of the really valuable oil.

Sweet waters were also made from lavender and from orange flowers but rose water was the favourite – Elizabeth I one year paid the large sum of £40 to 'stillers of sweet waters', a husband and wife named Kraunkewell. Rose water was used not only as a perfume but to sprinkle on floors and linen and to freshen clothes which could not be laundered easily. It was also a common ingredient in many dishes both sweet and savoury, often replacing doubtful well or stream water, and was used in wealthy households for rinsing hands after eating. By the beginning of the sixteenth century sweet waters were distilled in quite elaborate ways using a large pot or still which was heated by a brick-built furnace underneath. A domed head or alembic caught the steam and the distilled droplets ran through a beak-shaped pipe from the alembic to a container. There are many illustrations from this period, mostly from Europe, showing the distillation of flower waters and usually the still stands outside in a herb and flower garden which provides the raw ingredients for the process.

ABOVE Dry some complete rose heads as well as trays of petals. These can be added later to decorate a bowl of pot-pourri or used as they are to make a more textured mixture. If you grow plenty of garden roses, you can spare some complete rose buds to make a lovely addition to the finished mixture. Florist roses dry well but normally lack any kind of scent which might be retained after drying.

At the end of the summer, when you have a good collection of dried rose petals, you can begin to mix a decorative dry pot-pourri or make scented mixtures to fill sachets and bags. To help the mixture retain its scent, you must add powdered orris root or another similar fixative. Whole or ground spices are another essential ingredient and a few drops of a pure flower oil will bring the fragrance alive. Sticks or curls of cinnamon bark make a decorative addition as well as adding a spicey, warm scent. Other whole spices which can be added for the effect are whole nutmegs, with or without their mace covering, allspice, star anise, coriander, ginger root, and peppercorns.

The Tudor mixture of petals, herbs and powdered spices was put into small fabric bags and used in a very functional way. The term 'pot-pourri' was not used until the eighteenth century when the fragrant mixture was presented in beautiful china containers, with appearance as important as scent.

MOIST POT-POURRI RECIPE

10 cups scented rose petals
2 cups coarse non-iodized salt
1 cup dried lavender
1 cup dried lemon verbena leaves
4 tablespoons orris root powder
1 tablespoon ground nutmeg
1 tablespoon ground allspice
1 teaspoon ground cloves
Few drops rose essential oil

Dry roses until leathery. Layer petals with salt in a deep crock or bowl. Weigh mixture down with a plate and weight. Stir and mix daily for about two weeks. When the mixture is dry, crumble it and add the other ingredients. If the scent is not strong enough add a few drops of rose oil. Put into paper bags, seal and leave to cure in a cool dark place for about six weeks. Put into jars or lidded baskets and open when you need to. To make it decorative, scatter some whole dried flowers over it or add texture with whole spices and seeds.

Flowers in an Interior

From the evidence of inventories of the period it seems that people living in country houses of the sixteenth century enjoyed a higher standard of living and far greater comfort in terms of household furnishings and furniture than previously. This improvement in living conditions found its way down to farmers and skilled artisans and to merchant classes who benefitted greatly from a thriving import of luxury goods from Europe and beyond. William Harrison, in his contemporary description of England, claimed that:

> 'In the houses of knights, gentlemen, merchantmen and other wealthy citizens, it is not uncommon to behold generally their great provision of tapestry, Turkey work, pewter, fine linen, brass and thereto costly cupboards of plate . . . [and] it is now descended yet lower, even unto the inferior artificers and many farmers, who have for the most part also learnt to garnish their cupboards with plate, their joint beds with tapestry and silk hangings, and their tables with carpets and fine napery, whereby the wealth of our country . . . doth infinitely appear.'

BELOW The first spring blooms have a fleeting freshness and delicacy. Rosemary is one of the first herbs to flower and after a mild winter can be covered in soft dusky mauve blooms in April or even earlier. It has always been one of the commonest herbs to be grown and although, in Britain, it is not used very often in cooking, sprigs of rosemary have always found their way into bouquets for weddings, where it symbolizes fidelity, and into funeral wreaths, where it suggests remembrance.

There was a great fashion for decoration and 'anticke' ornament based on natural forms of birds, beasts and fishes, flowers, fruit and vegetables. Interior ceilings, walls and woodwork were often painted in black and white with quite simple and heavy designs incorporating trails of vines, cornucopia, dogs or dolphins. Panels of decoration were let into walls and around doors, above windows or on pillars and many materials were used including terracotta and stone. Exquisite embroidered hangings for beds and walls were carefully sewn, and petit point and tapestry of all kinds were used to cover seats and cushions or simply as pictures or samplers of stitches. Much of the work of this period is delightful and very fanciful, smothered with strange heraldic beasts and odd and peculiar insects, birds and flowers. Bible stories are sometimes the theme for the design or it could simply be a catalogue of varieties of plants and animals local to the area. Flowers are always strongly represented as they have been in embroidery throughout history.

Paintings of interiors and portraits of the period give us few clues as to how fresh flowers might have been used inside houses and the flower paintings of this time tended to show a catalogue of flower varieties rather than a representation of an arrangement of blooms in a vase. The early period of Dutch flower painting, which included artists such as Jan Bruegel the Elder who was working towards the very end of the sixteenth century, produced the first of the elaborate and detailed set-piece flower paintings that are very familiar to us now (see page 51). The subject was usually a mass of different blooms arranged to face the viewer against a rich, dark background. Little else apart from the vase and the flowers was included, except perhaps a few loose blooms or small objects lying on the surface beside the flowers.

We cannot presume, however, that flowers were arranged in this way to decorate interiors. Although the idea of a waterproof container seems to have been adopted by now to preserve the life of the cut stems, by looking closely at the painted flowers it is obvious that they span a whole season of flowering. Crown imperials bloom alongside poppies and hyacinth with autumn cyclamen, and they are simply a wonderful decorative fantasy dreamed up by the artist to celebrate the diversity and beauty of plant material available to him. The Netherlands was very much a centre for the trade in plants throughout the world and often these elaborate paintings were used to show off and describe one particular choice new introduction such as a tulip owned by a collector. Following on from these early paintings a slightly different style evolved through the seventeenth and eighteenth centuries and flower painting gradually became a genre in its own right.

The fruit and flower still life was a popular subject for paintings of this period. Exquisite summer fruits and perfect vegetable specimens were painted with loving detail, either alone or arranged with flowers. This arrangement of a bowl of plums and morning glory flowers is based on a delicate Italian painting by Giovanni Garzoni (1600–1670). His original includes ripe yellow plums with jasmine flowers and convolvulus, with broken fresh walnuts on the surface below. Here, bloom-covered dessert plums are piled into a shallow dish and scattered with white mallow flowers. The convolvulus are almost a flight of fancy as they last for such a brief time, but the whole arrangement would make a perfect centrepiece for a summer dinner as decoration and dessert combined.

Tulipa suavéolens

CHAPTER THREE

THE FORMAL GARDEN

FROM RESTORATION TO ROMANTICISM

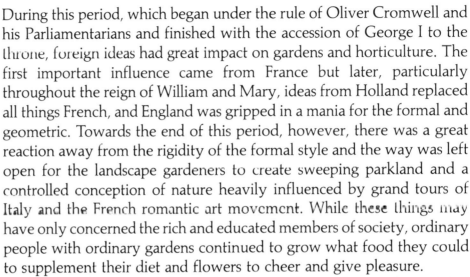

During this period, which began under the rule of Oliver Cromwell and his Parliamentarians and finished with the accession of George I to the throne, foreign ideas had great impact on gardens and horticulture. The first important influence came from France but later, particularly throughout the reign of William and Mary, ideas from Holland replaced all things French, and England was gripped in a mania for the formal and geometric. Towards the end of this period, however, there was a great reaction away from the rigidity of the formal style and the way was left open for the landscape gardeners to create sweeping parkland and a controlled conception of nature heavily influenced by grand tours of Italy and the French romantic art movement. While these things may have only concerned the rich and educated members of society, ordinary people with ordinary gardens continued to grow what food they could to supplement their diet and flowers to cheer and give pleasure.

This was the time of the tussie-mussie, when judges and convicted criminals alike, ever mindful of the ravages of plague, carried small bunches of flowers and herbs in a vain attempt to protect themselves from disease, and flower sellers shouted from street corners offering the little posies for sale. New plants arrived in the country in a steady stream, collected from North and South America, and from East India and the West Indies via Holland.

A neat bunch of shiny green box leaves suggests the topiary art of a formal Jacobean garden.

Gardens on a Grand Scale

By 1664 the word parterre had succeeded knot garden and the design of gardens had undergone a change. There were now experts on gardening and horticulture, books were written on the subject, wealthy landowners employed designers and nurserymen to lay out fabulous gardens on a scale not seen before. Everyone who could afford such grand ideas wished to own a garden like the ones laid out by the French designer-in-ordinary Le Notre, who spent his life planning and planting gardens on a magnificent scale including Louis XIV's palace grounds at Versailles and whose influence dominated European gardening at this time.

At one point Charles II tried to obtain the services of Le Notre for his royal gardens but it is doubtful that he ever came and worked in England, although two famous English gardeners, John Rose and George London, both visited France and Rose learned directly from Le Notre. This French style of gardening took elements of the European Renaissance garden and added enormously long avenues, sweeping vistas and immense acreages of trees laid out in geometric patterns crisscrossed by paths and areas of water. Everything was planned with mathematical accuracy and precision and suited the flat landscape of many parts of northern France. Translated to England it was not always as successful and expensive

BELOW & RIGHT The sophistication of the formal garden, with hedges and plants used in a purely architectural way, meant that flowers and colour were banished to specific parts of the the garden leaving the simplicity of texture and materials to speak louder than individual plants. The gardens at Peover Hall in Cheshire have a landscaped park laid out in the eighteenth century as well as five walled gardens and nineteenth-century additions.

LEFT While the style of the pleasure garden of the grand country house changed over the centuries, the walled kitchen garden remained a practical area, designed to produce all the fruit, vegetables, herbs and flowers the house might need throughout the year. It also made a highly decorative and pleasant place for recreation, as gravel paths kept feet dry even after rain and there was always an interest in the development of special fruit and flowers. Many varieties of fruit tree respond well to being trained – as here, where apple trees are grown as cordons over arches along a gravel walk in an eighteenth-century walled garden.

construction work such as that needed for canals and water features were often scaled down to a smaller budget.

While there were still areas of parterre which needed to be filled with brightly coloured flowers for the best effect, it was very much a time of greenery, trees and garden structure. This explains perhaps why some flowers assumed a special position of importance and were grown as curiosities and show pieces to be displayed in elaborate plant theatres. Ranunculus, tulips, auriculas and dianthus all had this treatment and came to be known as florist flowers. Florist then meant someone who grew and bred flowers, rather than a seller of flowers.

In 1664 a very influential book was published. *Sylva, or a Discourse of Forest Trees* was written by the royalist John Evelyn at the request of the Royal Society in order

BELOW A kitchen garden does not have to be four acres of walled land, carefully tended by an army of gardeners to produce flowers, fruit and vegetables for the house. These days it seems sensible to grow those things which are difficult to find in shops and which must be fresh to be worth having. A small patch of garden kept to grow flowers for picking is an old-fashioned idea but one worth reviving. A few packets of seeds of annual flowers such as cornflowers, larkspur and sweet peas will fill jugs and vases all through the summer with the plants which they produce. You could add a rose bush or two for a constant supply of petals and flowers, and maybe dianthus plants which would need very little maintenance. One biennial plant which is well worth growing is the sweet william, which produces masses of blooms over several weeks in early summer and the flowers last beautifully in water.

to counteract the gradual destruction of England's forests and to encourage new tree planting. Evelyn also wrote a *Gard'ners Almanac* which was the first gardeners' calendar to be published in England. He is credited with being a great proponent of the Lebanon cedar, although it had already been introduced and recorded, and he appears to have been influential in making the common yew a more popular garden plant for hedges and topiary work than the widely used box.

About the same time that Evelyn's books were being published, another gardening author, John Rea, published his work entitled *Flora, Ceres and Pomona . . . or a complete Florilege, furnished with all requisites belonging to a florist*. This book contains an insight into gardens laid out on a less grandiose scale, which might be found up and down the country in rural areas. He describes how to build and plant a garden for 'delight, recreation and entertainment' to the south of the house, one half for flowers and the other principally for fruit. The kitchen garden, he says, should be in some more remote place as it was not considered to be decorative. His instructions for planting fruit trees, such as pears and pomegranates, on walls amongst standard rose trees implies that they were grown ornamentally for their blossom as well as productively for their fruit. Rea describes borders below the fruit trees containing a wonderful mix of flowers including red primrose, hepaticas, double rose campions, auriculas, double dame's violet, wallflowers and double stock gillyflowers which must have smelt delicious in the sheltered and enclosed garden.

An important part of any garden at this time was the 'greens' planted in pots. This practice began around 1660 and by 1690 one of the most important elements in a well-furnished garden was the quality and quantity of different greens whose foliage had to be 'bright'. Evergreen plants such as myrtle, orange and lemon were

LEFT The fashion for clipped evergreens and topiary was at its height during this period. It is possible to sculpt small box or yew shapes in just a few years. To create a topiary garden of this size needs patience, space and commitment and a steady hand and eye when it comes to giving the bushes their annual clip, so it is probably best to begin with a single specimen in a pot or tub for practice before turning to more grandiose plans such as these at Parnham House in Dorset.

ABOVE To create a piece of topiary allow the plant to grow and fill out well, loosely trimming any over-long branches. Once the plant is approaching the height and width you need, begin to clip into the desired shape. Use small hand shears for the closest cut and tidy the shape every few months or as it is needed. Eventually, the leaves should get very dense and the outline will just need regular shaving to keep it crisp and in order. Feed pot-grown plants with a slow-release granular fertilizer or a liquid feed to keep the foliage lush and healthy. For the right period feel, use terracotta pots or wooden tubs.

stood outside in the summer and brought under cover during the cold winter months. Before the exact needs of plants were understood, tubs of evergreens were overwintered in unsuitable buildings with little ventilation and only a small amount of glass, but by the middle of the eighteenth century orangeries and greenhouses were entirely glazed and therefore far more conducive to healthy and flourishing plants. The word greenhouse comes from the use of 'green' as a shortened form of evergreen to describe the plants put in such a building.

The Dutch influence that permeated garden design following the accession of William (of Holland) and Mary to the throne in 1688 showed itself particularly in the fanciful and complicated designs for parterres and a tendency to concentrate on small detail, emphasizing an overall smaller scale of doing things. Bulbs of all kinds became the most fashionable plants to grow and they were perfectly suited to the bedding-out schemes and infilling of box-edged parterres. Statuary became a common garden feature and the art of topiary reached extraordinary heights. From simple cones and pyramids of clipped evergreens grew fantastic spirals, corkscrews, people and birds sculpted very often in box but also in privet, juniper and whitethorn, with yew only becoming popular later from the mid seventeenth century. By 1712 the excesses of man's interference with nature, epitomized in such pursuits as topiary, were beginning to be ridiculed by the literary minded such as Addison and Pope and slowly the tide turned on the formal ordered garden and a new vision was heralded – a romantic view and a celebration of the natural landscape.

The formal garden in the distance of this Breughel painting is divided into regular sized plots bounded by fences and paths. Nothing can be seen of the plants growing in this enclosed garden, but the flowers encircling the landscape give some idea of the varied plants which were available to the gardener during this period. As usual the seasons overlap so that apple blossom and sprays of laburnum bloom alongside roses, honeysuckle, jasmine, lilies, aconites, campanula and borage. The tulips and dianthus show the elaborate streaking and feathering which were the desirable qualities for a classic florist flower.

ABOVE Borage takes its name from the Celtic word *borrach*, meaning to have courage, because it was thought that an infusion of borage leaves gave the drinker this quality. It is still used to flavour and decorate summer drinks, and in Victorian times there were many recipes for cooling claret cups decorated with sprigs of jaunty blue borage flowers. Borage is a vigorous annual which will seed itself with abandon, but few people mind this intrusion and it saves the need to re-sow each year. The blue starry flowers with deep black eyes are unusual and highly decorative and deserve to be used more frequently in food and decorations.

•❖•

RIGHT The double daisy has a quiet charm which is often overlooked in the search for colour and dramatic impact. It is a well-loved plant, grown in English gardens since medieval times. Traditonally grown as a border or path edging, it mixes happily with spring bulbs, violas and pansies. Daisies are easy to grow from seed and in the right conditions are reliably perennial. There are several varieties to choose from, including Dresden China, Rob Roy and Pomponette, the one illustrated here.

Flowers of the Period
•❖•

The second half of the seventeenth century saw an enormous increase in the importation of tender and hardy plants. Both France and Holland were clearing houses for freshly found species and many ordinary people doing business in foreign countries brought back seeds or plants which they grew in their own gardens. There was a tremendous interest in all the 'exoticks' as they were known and nurserymen at this time went to great lengths to breed unusual and desirable plants. A nurseryman named Darby, who grew plants in Hoxton in London, propagated many different variegated silver and gold hollies which were very popular as greens for tubs and it was during this period that many nurseries experimented with hybridization and raising new varieties of quite common and well-loved plants. The records that survive are mostly of the London nurseries, of which there were many, but there must have been other nurseries near larger towns and well-populated areas.

The plants grown in cottage gardens would hardly have changed from the previous century so that primroses, gillyflowers and lilies were as popular as ever. Judging by one book of the period, wealthy and fashionable gardeners might have been able to select from over 190 varieties of tulip, but this was at the height of tulipomania. Other flowers found growing in a late seventeenth-century garden might have included narcissi, amaryllis, cyclamen, iris, crocus, colchicums, hyacinths, alliums and auriculas with names such as Mr Good's Purple or Rickett's Sable, named after the person who bred them. Summer flowering plants which were popular at the time included delphiniums, scabious, lupins, cornflowers, perennial sweet peas and mallows, all flowers we might expect to find in a herbaceous border today; and grown amongst the flowers were exotica such as tomatoes, known as 'love apples', which were used decoratively and not eaten.

Hemerocallis flava or day lily is a native of Central Europe and has been grown in gardens for centuries, although it is only since the nineteenth century and more recently in the last decade or two that much work on hybridizing has been done. Known at one point as an asphodel lily, it has roots similar to the asphodel and flowers like those of a lily. Each bloom lasts for just a day but there is a succession of flowers during July and August which makes the day lily such a useful garden plant. The original native version had yellow flowers but now there are varieties in all shades of yellow, orange, terracotta and deep rusty red.

RIGHT A display of spring garden flowers are laid out here like a botanical illustration. From left to right in rows starting at the top of the picture: The seed heads of *Helleborus corsicus*, a variegated strawberry leaf and flower, a chive flower, aquilegia Norah Barlow, honeysuckle Early Cream, Geranium Kashmir white, a single flower head of auricula, quince blossom, tulip with honesty flowers, white sweet violet, *Geranium renardii*, *Geranium phaeum*, pansies, *Ajuga reptans* Variegata. All these flowers would have been known and grown during the late seventeenth and early eighteenth centuries and are still popular two hundred years on. Fruit trees were appreciated for the beauty of their spring blossom, such as the apple here, just as much as for the usefulness of their fruit.

The variety of fruit during this period is quite remarkable and was obviously considered an important part of the aesthetic appeal of any garden. Perhaps this explains the use of fruit in still-life flower paintings of the period where translucent bunches of grapes or exquisitely perfect pears lie amongst the leaves and flowers on marble pillars. From books of the time come descriptions of 24 kinds of cherry, 5 kinds of quince, 20 kinds of pear, 44 varieties of plum, 6 of apricot or 'apricocks' as they were called and 35 varieties of peach. Also mentioned were figs, mulberries, medlars, sorbs, vines and nuts. Although this number of varieties was to be later surpassed it does show the sophistication and speed with which nurserymen and growers had developed these trees since medieval times.

Small cottage gardens would have had space for only a limited number of plants and precedence would have been given to herbs and medicinal flowers. New arrivals found their way surprisingly quickly into small gardens so that plants such as the crown imperial, *Fritillaria imperialis*, and tulips became cottage garden favourites in a short space of time. But mostly the simple and common plants formed the main collections amongst the jumble of fruit, herbs and vegetables that made up any country garden of this period. Flowers like forget-me-nots, violets, bluebells and honesty, all easy to grow, hardy and good natured, survived the passion for greens, clipped edges and gravel walks and quietly remained growing in the English country garden.

Florist Flowers

LEFT The auricula was one of the most prized and talked-about flowers of this period. We have the choice these days of growing either the simpler garden varieties or the more elaborate show types which have come back into fashion over the last decade. As long as it is remembered that the auricula is an alpine plant which can withstand low temperatures but does not relish damp conditions, then these plants are quite easy to grow. Single and double alpine types, which come in a range of many different colours, are quite happy grown outdoors in a sheltered and well-drained border or raised bed. They can be cut to make lovely flowers for indoor arrangements and last well in water. The scent of auriculas is fresh and delicious and very similar to that of wild cowslips. All varieties can be grown in pots and, as here, a collection of several different types and colours can be arranged in a basket, surrounded with moss, to be brought indoors and enjoyed while they are in flower.

RIGHT There are many paintings from the seventeenth and eighteenth centuries of florist flowers, especially of the auricula which was an extremely decorative subject for any flower painter. The neat and organized head of blooms set upon a stiff, straight stem suited the fashion for symmetry and order. Show varieties of auriculas are still grown in pots to protect them from too much rain which spoils the white dusty meal on the leaves and flowers.

By the mid seventeenth century particular flowers became extremely important as they were taken up and developed by the florists. The carnation, ranunculus, anemone and tulip were the first to receive this special treatment, followed a little later by the auricula, hyacinth, polyanthus and the pink. Other flowers were added as the years progressed and by the nineteenth century pansies and dahlias became classic florist flowers.

Florist in this case meant someone who grew fine flowers and exhibited them, often competing against other florists and forming groups of like-minded growers to meet or hold feasts. In the seventeenth century the art of growing florist flowers was confined to people of wealth, while the later nineteenth-century florists were mainly urban-dwelling industrial workers. Flowers which were considered worthy of special treatment had to have certain qualities. The outline of the flower should be circular if possible, the stem stiff to hold the flower well, and some colour variegation was desirable.

The auricula was one of the first florist flowers which remained important and is

now enjoying a renaissance. In the wild, auriculas thrive in alpine conditions but the garden varieties, which first appeared in the mid sixteenth century, were probably hybrids with other primula species. Auriculas had the neat habit and stylized looks of a clipped topiary tree and suited the seventeenth-century taste for plants which exhibited implicit obedience. The early auriculas were commonly striped and only later came to display the very pronounced and organized markings that we recognize now, with rings of colour and distinct edgings. Auriculas are curious flowers with their dusting of white meal over the petals and the neat organization of a bunch of flowers on a single stem all flowering at the same time and in the same state of perfection. For the florists they epitomized nature under control and as well as possessing an almost unreal beauty they had the added attraction of a sublime scent very similar to the scent of cowslips.

Another flower which attracted the attention of the seventeenth-century florists was the hyacinth, which arrived in Western Europe from the Ottoman Empire during the mid sixteenth century. The original species was a graceful curving plant similar to the English native bluebell but it changed out of all recognition in the hands of the florists and plant breeders. The hyacinth, like the auricula, possessed a strong scent and began life blue, or occasionally white. By the early eighteenth century double-flowered forms appeared and the whole shape of the flower altered with the stem shrinking and the flowers therefore closer together. Hyacinths regularly appeared in the elaborate flower paintings of the time which often showed the single and double varieties together. They reached their peak of popularity in the eighteenth century when there were 2000 cultivars to choose from, and at one stage bulbs of certain varieties were more expensive than the treasured tulips. Madame de Pompadour had hyacinths bedded out in their thousands at Versailles because she adored their scent, but the florists and hyacinth fanciers were more likely to have grown the flowers individually in pots or glasses as 'their roots were a most diverting pleasure to behold'.

Nowadays we have little choice in hyacinths. They are mostly of the same type, a rather squat and stubby shape, hardly tapering at all, while the best scent is found in the more open and loose-flowered Roman hyacinths or multi-flora varieties as they are usually called. We can still enjoy them growing in water-filled hyacinth glasses standing on a windowsill, and although the original root glasses of the eighteenth century may be far too expensive to use, there are modern versions which look every bit as pretty as the antique ones.

At the beginning of the eighteenth century there appeared notices of florists' feasts, forerunners of today's horticultural shows. The feasts were usually held in public houses in spring and summer. The flowers were displayed either cut or in pots, and prizes, often silver spoons, were presented to the winner. After the flowers were judged, a good meal was eaten and the flowers were later passed round the table and discussed when everyone was in mellow mood.

•◄►•

Popular flowering bulbs during this period included the hyacinth, which was sometimes planted outside in a colourful mass and sometimes as a single specimen in a pot or special glass. Grown in a hyacinth glass, the bulb simply sent roots down into water and the flower bloomed as it might outdoors. This method is still used today and is a pretty and decorative way of having scented flowers in the house during the winter. Look out for hyacinth vases which are often available when the bulbs are sold for planting in the early autumn. Many other small bulbs are suitable for growing in pots for indoor use. Choose from winter- and spring-flowering crocus, miniature narcissi and species daffodils, many of the small early flowering iris, such as *Iris reticulata* or *danfordiae*, and scilla, *Anemone blanda* and grape hyacinth.

Indoor Flowers

‹—›

While there is no doubt that flowers were grown with a passion and enthusiasm which sparked off such happenings as florists' feasts, we cannot be sure what place flowers had in the interiors of this time. Grand houses of the period had space and light enough to show off vases of fragrant flowers and we can only presume that they did. Flowers were always in fashion and portraits of the time show flowers tucked into a neckline or hat, edging a dress or simply held in the hand. Posies to carry were commonplace and flowers still played an important part in scenting clothes, linens and furniture and were made into fragrant sweet waters and perfumes. *Hesperis tristis*, a variety of sweet rocket or dame's violet, is

RIGHT A sophisticated garland made from dried leaves and other plant material has echoes of eighteenth-century wood carving. To make this wreath you will need a dried vine ring on which to build up the layers of leaves, nuts and dried flowers. Choose glossy brown *Magnolia grandiflora* leaves or laurel leaves, and glue these onto the vine wreath, ideally using a glue gun which is quick and efficient. Use one large and important seedhead or pine cone at the bottom of the ring together with one or two other interesting pieces such as dried globe artichoke flower heads. Fill in with lighter weight material such as dried hydrangea florets and maple or sycamore leaves, and add pecan nuts, almonds, brazils or hazelnuts in their shells until you have a pleasing balance of shapes and textures. Hang the finished garland on a door or wall or above a fireplace, or lay it flat as a table decoration, if you prefer.

‹—›

‹—›

LEFT Some small and rather precious plants, such as this Garryarde Guinevere primrose, can be more easily cosseted when grown in a pot, away from the crowding and confusion of the mixed herbaceous border. In their natural state, primroses and polyanthus prefer woodland conditions with plenty of moisture and humidity. During spring they relish sunshine, but later in the year they are happiest in a shady or semi-shady place where they will not dry out too much. A pot can be moved around to suit the seasonal conditions, and can even be brought indoors for a few days when the flowers are at their best.

thought to have been grown in pots to stand and scent bedrooms with its heady evening fragrance, and mignonette, though a very unshowy plant, was potted up for the same purpose and stood in windowsills to freshen and sweeten the air in a room. In 1700 the Duchess of Beaufort had a special stove-house built at Badminton for her collection of exotic and tender plants. Presumably some of these plants, when flowering or at their best, were brought into the house itself.

As in previous centuries, flowers were very much part of all celebrations and festivals and were used lavishly at weddings and church occasions. The *Origins of Ancient Customs*, dated 1672, says 'No-one questions the propriety of a chaplet of roses for newly-married people, seeing that flowers in general and roses in particular are sacred to Venus, to the Graces and to Love'. Mayday was also full of

The practice of making small posies of flowers and herbs called tussie mussies has survived since medieval times. During the seventeenth century, judges and lawyers, fearful of coming into contact with the plague from prisoners in court, carried small bunches of herbs, and rosemary and rue were scattered on the floors of the courtroom. Around the beginning of the eighteenth century, the Recorder of the City of London carried a posy made from seven specific herbs that were thought to protect the carrier from infectious diseases. The bunch illustrated here has been made using these seven herbs: camomile, lemon balm, rue, marjoram, lavender, sage and hyssop. Sometimes roses or wallflowers were added too.

LEFT Jan van Huysum (1682–1749) painted some of the most beautiful flower still lifes of this period. While his paintings were accurate and detailed catalogues of particular flowers, they were also exquisite compositions in their own right. Here a classic terracotta urn on a marble ledge contains roses, a red peony, a deep, almost black iris, a single marigold beside a stem of larkspur, dianthus, a tulip and a subtly-coloured auricula. Tumbling from the vase are a spray of blue campanulas and three flowers of the annual *Convolvulus tricolor*.

RIGHT There is a point in the year, usually at the beginning of June, when the flower garden is in transition from spring to summer flowers and there is an extraordinary variety of blooms to pick. It is then possible to re-create a flower still-life arrangement which looks very like an old flower painting of the seventeenth or eighteenth century. The mixture of very bright colours in great quantity might seem disastrous but, if enough different flowers are used, the whole arrangement does come together and each flower is important in its own right while contributing to the overall design.

Choose old-fashioned garden flowers such as brilliant poppies, stocks, foxgloves, vivid nasturtiums, sweet peas and cornflowers and do not be tempted to use foliage as a filler. Aim to leave clear spaces around each flower so that they can be seen individually and, if possible, arrange each stem to face forwards. Use a classic vase, such as this black Wedgwood urn, to complete the feel, and continue the still life beneath the vase by placing a few pieces of beautiful fruit on the table. A stem or two of twining curvy leaves and flowers, such as clematis or rose, can be left to fall naturally from the vase to the table.

flowers which were used to decorate garlands and to twine round the tree used as a Maypole, while all the people involved would wear flowers as decoration on their clothes and round their heads and hats.

The flower paintings of this period are a wonderful guage of which flower species were grown but tell us less about how flowers were arranged and used inside house. The detailed and richly-coloured paintings are very much studio pieces, making use of controlled and often unnatural lighting effects, and the flowers are arranged on the canvas in such a way as to make them all look magnificent. There is little sense of place or mood but instead one has perfect draughtsmanship, a magnificent use of colour and fine observation of nature. The backgrounds of these paintings were invariably as dark as possible to throw the shapes and colours into relief and did not usually portray a realistic corner of a room. The stronghold of flower painting during this period was Holland and Flanders and this remained the case until well into the nineteenth century when France took over as the country producing many of the finest floral artists.

CHAPTER FOUR

PARADISE AND PERFECTION

THE GEORGIAN IDEAL

Georgian Britain saw an unprecedented sophistication in all the arts. It was the time of the great country house and estate, when a rising class of industrialists and those made rich in India and North America sought power and position through building or buying a fine house and land. The old system of agriculture, which was based on one man farming different strips of land which could be quite a distance apart, changed under the enclosure laws. Larger fields were created, bounded by streams or an existing road or copse, and a single crop was grown in the larger space. Following the contours of the land, this made the patchwork of countryside we are familiar with today.

The landscape was to become all important. Gardeners gave way to landscape artists who had, in Alexander Pope's famous phrase, to 'consult the genius of the place in all'. Nature became revered – in art, poetry and literature. The straight lines and avenues, clipped trees and parterres were considered old fashioned and out of keeping with the new spirit, whereas ha-ha's, follies and grottoes were much in favour along with artificial ruins, gothic temples and hermits' cells. In formal gardens flowers may have had to remain in the background for a time but they appeared everywhere else in abundance. Introductions from abroad continued apace and glasshouses could not be built fast enough.

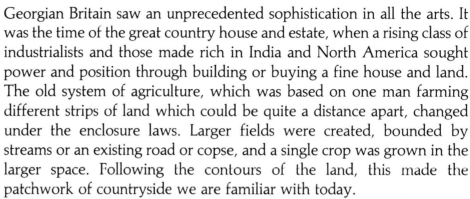

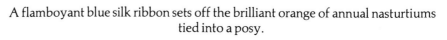

A flamboyant blue silk ribbon sets off the brilliant orange of annual nasturtiums tied into a posy.

The Landscape Garden

The eighteenth century was a time for frivolous flowers and flowers used in a generous and frivolous way. While in many grand gardens the flowers were swept from view into a walled corner, they continued to flourish away from the landscaped parkland and found their way indoors to delight the taste for the romantic. Tulips have gone in and out of fashion many times in their history. From their heyday in the seventeenth century they have always been a wonderful standby for making colour in the late spring garden, and they have become something of a cliche in municipal bedding schemes, combined with forget-me-nots and wallflowers. Tulips are now enjoying another revival, with many people choosing soft colours rather than screaming scarlet, and pretty shaped flowers such as the lily-flowered varieties and the exotic frilled and cut-edged parrot tulips. Here a taller white variety has been planted with a shorter peony-flowered, pink Angelique tulip and a sprinkling of wild blue-bells.

Love of the country was to become the fashionable style of the day. Town houses were necessary for those who could afford them but the estate set in magnificent parkland and with no neighbour in view was the ultimate aim of a man of style and success. Achieving this aim often incurred a great loss of productive farm land and enormous expense in the creation of the undulating grassland, curving lakes and 'natural' woods and stony outcrops necessary to produce the perfect landscape. The country house and parkland were set in the countryside but separated from it by the building of a trench which had a retaining wall and sunken fence within it to keep animals on the right side. This device came to be known as a ha-ha and was crucial to the creation of the idyllic sweeping vistas demanded by the garden designers and architects of the day.

While designers like Charles Bridgeman were thinking on a stupendously large scale for clients such as George II, men like Batty Langley, who lived and worked at Twickenham, spoke to those of smaller means through books such as *The New Principles of Gardening* published in 1728. His designs for gardens tended still to be geometric but he suggested that flowers could be grown in little thickets or clusters, seemingly without order and not in the straight rows popular hitherto.

The great parks and gardens laid out for the grand and wealthy by landscapers such as Humphrey Repton and Capability Brown have tended to obscure the history of smaller gardens of the period and the ways that flowers were grown in them. The rural cottage garden, the vicarage garden and those attached to middle-sized houses in provincial towns would probably have changed little in design. Judging by the catalogues from nurseries at the time, however, ordinary people were buying flower plants in large quantities from a superb choice of varieties.

William Cobbett, famous for his *Rural Rides*, also wrote books on gardens. In *The English Gardener*, he gives much space to the cultivation of flowers although his great interest was always in growing vegetables, fruit and other productive food crops. Interestingly, the longest paragraphs on flowers cover the ever popular florist flowers – anemones, ranunculus, pinks, auricula, hyacinths, tulips and carnations. Other writers gave instructions, with a careful eye to colour scheming, on the layout of borders containing mixed flowers which would all bloom at the same time, and it would appear that by about 1770 the flower garden as we think of it today had more or less developed. Up until now flowers had generally been grown in plots containing a single type of bloom, but with the advent of more natural serpentine flower beds cut into lawn and the use of flowers to edge groups of trees and shrubs, the emphasis was now on painting an area of colour and shape using plants as the medium.

Even in the large naturalistic parkland gardens there was always a kitchen garden to produce fruit, vegetables and flowers for the household. Here flowers were grown as specimens and also specifically for picking. In 1757 Sir John Hill published a book called *The Flower Garden* in which he suggests that while flowers should be grown in what he calls the Pleasure Garden there should also be a Flower Garden, a 'particular piece of Ground for the Beds of select kinds'. So while flowers and colour were being banished from the larger landscape view, they were being used to create a harmonious effect in the smaller garden.

LEFT In the garden of Cranborne Manor in Dorset, which was part laid out by John Tradescant in the seventeenth century and has been developed ever since, translucent tulips are lit up by the low spring sunshine. Brilliant red tulips have naturalized in grass alongside buttercups and the remains of narcissi. This treatment is natural and effective and a total contrast to the stiff and aritificial plantings of tulips in serried rows.

One contemporary description of a pleasure garden describes groves of evergreens mixed with flowering shrubs, and some large trees for shade. Spring flowers such as crocus, hyacinth, violets, primroses, daffodils and daisies bloom in the grass in spring and some of the tall stemmed trees have plants growing round them, many of them sweetly scented. The list includes roses, sweet briars, honeysuckles, sweet peas, nasturtiums and, interestingly, scarlet runner beans grown for their looks rather than food.

The skills of the gardener needed to be increased and updated all the time as new and challenging plants continued to be introduced from abroad. Many tender plants such as dahlias, zinnias and cosmos came from Mexico and needed special treatment in order to survive the cold damp winters in Britain. The first official

BELOW A glorious jewel-like mix of colours light up a spring garden. Deep rusty-orange wallflowers fill a long kitchen garden border, fronted by drifts of deep blue forget-me-nots, the whole stretch dotted with tulips and late pheasant eye narcissi. On one side is an ancient, rosemary plant in full bloom and, above it all, apple and pear blossom in abundance with espalier-trained fruit trees and cordon trees growing over an arch.

collector for Kew gardens brought back many sun-loving plants from South Africa including crinums, nerines and agapanthus. These new plants had to be recorded and drawn, and serious collectors like Mary Somerset, Duchess of Beaufort, commissioned botanical illustrators who made many exquisite drawings and paintings which remain to this day. These were among the first in a long line of important records of botanical specimens and still today flowers are recorded by accurate drawing and painting rather than by photography.

In 1730 the first highly-illustrated nursery catalogue was published for the famous nurseries of Robert Furber in Kensington, London. Called *Twelve Months of Flowers*, it contained twelve plates of hand-coloured engravings, showing flowers for each month. No prices were mentioned.

One very important artist of this period, who did much to raise the standard of botanical illustration in Europe was Georg Dionysius Ehret, a German who came to

LEFT Here a collection of summer garden flowers is laid out like a botanical illustration. Illustrators of flowers during the eighteenth century often arranged the specimens in a highly decorative way, making use of devices such as twisted and flowing ribbons to turn a simple illustration into a charming flower picture. Here three varieties of flower have been chosen for this treatment. The tall yellow thistle-type flower is *Centaurea macrocephela*, an easily-grown hardy perennial. There are also a blue and a white version of nigella or love-in-a-mist beside a deep crimson dianthus.

•❖•

•❖•

RIGHT Hollyhocks were mentioned in a poem of the fifteenth century and have been common flowers ever since then, standing guard beside old walls and cottage doors and forming part of everyone's romantic view of a cottage garden. They are native to the Near East and it is said that the Crusaders called them hollyhocks from the word colly or cabbage, which referred to the doubling of the flower. By 1650 there were dozens of named varieties, both single and double, in a large colour range spanning white, pink, cream, yellow, red, maroon and salmon. They are simple to raise from seed and perennial, and although they are very prone to rust disease and mildew, they are invariably worth the time and effort spent on their cultivation.

live in England in 1735. He spent much time travelling through the country, stopping off to visit gardens and plant collections and recording new plants which he found. A gardener by training, Ehret was a natural artist who began making botanical drawings for his own satisfaction. His work became very popular, and he was in great demand to teach drawing in fashionable and aristocratic circles. He met the naturalist Linnaeus in Holland and they collaborated on *Hortus Cliffordiunus*, an illustrated catalogue of all the plants in the garden of George Clifford, a wealthy financier who lived at Hartekamp in Holland. Ehret was a competent exponent of Linnaeus's plant classification system and provided many drawings for various publications. His work has a superb accuracy and seriousness, combined with a fresh and lightness of touch and sense of design.

A rose is a rose is a rose . . . but it is not as simple as that. You can buy original old varieties and also new breeds designed to look like the old roses, as well as the many true species which are as they grow in the wild. This selection of roses, all from one garden, includes types from many rose categories. Working from left to right and starting at the *top row*: Canary Bird, Comte de Chambord, Baron Girod de L'Ain, Seagull. *2nd row*: Blanc Double de Coubert, Variegata de Bologna, *Rosa moyesii* Geranium, Felicite Parmentier. *3rd row*: Reine des Violettes, Felicia, *Rosa fedtschenkoana*, Old Blush China, English Rose Graham Thomas.

The Flowering of the Rose

The rose came into its own as a decorative flower during this period, filling gardens with its scent and covering fabrics and porcelain with its beauty. It had long been a favourite flower in every kind of garden but towards the end of the eighteenth century and in the early nineteenth century the introduction of new species from China led to a tremendous growth in rose breeding. Two of the most influential newcomers were Hume's Blush Tea-scented China and the Yellow Tea-scented China which was to be such an important colour in the breeding of new roses. The significance of all the new introductions was that the plants had more than one flowering period and by crossing them with other varieties it began to be possible to have roses which continued to flower right through the summer. From approximately 21 varieties of rose available in 1660 the number grew in an astonishing fashion so that by 1836 one famous nursery could offer 24 moss roses, 25 Provence or cabbage roses, 50 perpetual roses, 89 hybrid China roses, 25 alba roses, 19 damask roses, 99 gallica roses, 53 climbing roses, 70 China roses, 16 miniature China roses, 66 noisette roses, 38 Bourbon roses, 10 musk roses, 54 species and unclassified roses.

LEFT *Rosa sulfurea*, painted by Pierre Joseph Redoute (1759–1840), was one of the collection of roses owned by the Empress Josephine in her garden at Malmaison in France. Redoute painted all the roses she grew, but sadly Josephine died before the book was completed. While she sent collectors all over the world to find new roses for her collection, the Empress was spurred on by a rival rose lover, the Countess of Bougainville, who was also amassing as many varieties as possible. Little wonder that the rose became the most important flower in France at this time.

Much of the revived interest in roses must have come from the Empress Josephine, Napoleon's wife, who collected together at Malmaison in France the largest number of different roses ever grown in one place. She also encouraged the breeding of new varieties and commissioned Pierre-Joseph Redoute to paint a collection of roses which was published as *Les Roses* between 1817 and 1824. He was a brilliant flower painter who in turn worked for the court under Marie Antoinette, saw the French Revolution end the reign of the Bourbons, and then worked through Napoleon's rise and fall.

Flowers of the Period

All the favourite flowers remained in the cottage garden, with some of the fashionable new varieties filtering down via seed or cutting from the manor house or vicarage garden. The florist flowers also stayed much as they had been although the mania for tulips had waned and generally the interest in growing show blooms was being taken up by ordinary people. As more and more people moved from villages to work in towns or to work at a machine rather than on the land, growing a few pots of pinks or auriculas provided a hobby in complete contrast to an indoor repetitive job. The early nineteenth century was the golden age of the pink, and plantsmen's lists show a choice of up to 192 varieties bred by well-known florists such as Barlow, Keen and Hogg. The colliers of Durham and Northumberland and workers along Tyneside and Teesdale all grew show pinks but one group of workers became renowned for the growing of laced pinks. These

RIGHT This anonymous nineteenth-century painting shows an unnamed pink with the typical colouring and patterning of one of the old laced varieties, very similar to Murray's laced pink. Only recently does there seem to have been an interest in reviving these beautiful old varieties and the National collection of pinks is held in a private garden in Oxfordshire.

LEFT & RIGHT The peony is an ancient plant and one which came into cultivation very early on in garden history. French hybridizers in the early nineteenth century took various scented peonies, some Chinese introductions and the original *Peony officinalis*, and created many new and magnificent varieties. The single peonies are far more subtle than their blowsy double cousins, but both types deserve space in a garden which has room for them. They need good soil and plenty of humus and are happy in sun and partial shade. They take a few years to settle and grow to a good size, but will then repay with a spectacular show of flowers. The display is all too brief, but fabulous while it lasts for the two weeks or so during early summer.

were the weavers of Paisley near Glasgow in Scotland who led hard-working and strict Presbyterian lives, weaving fine paisley fabrics and shawls. From show and nursery catalogues we know they tended plants of beautifully marked and patterned pinks, but unfortunately we have no plants left or even illustrations to describe exactly how these flowers looked, although old varieties of laced pink have reappeared from other parts of the country since those days. The weavers also grew some tulips and carnations – at one 'Annual and Amicable Competition' 300 varieties of pheasant eye carnations, 80 types of laced pink and 200 varieties of tulip were shown.

Carnations continued to be grown with great enthusiasm and at the beginning of the nineteenth century the plant was divided into three distinct types called flakes, bizarres and picotees. All three moved in and out of fashion within the space of a few decades. The popularity of the carnation and the ease by which it could be bred and adapted led to the rejection of many varieties when a new one came along. There are few if any of these nineteenth-century varieties surviving today but there are some very ancient breeds of pink which are still grown. Another florist flower which is now only grown commercially as a cut flower and rarely seen in gardens is the ranunculus. Between 1815 and 1820 English florists began to raise many new varieties from seed, producing wonderful new colour combinations and edgings, and the flower seemed as popular as it had been during the eighteenth century. By 1860, however, it ceased to be of any importance and declined from then on.

William Cobbett lists the most wonderful choice of flowers in *The English Gardener*, and explains simply but with expertise how to grow each plant. According to him, only the florists cultivate their choice specimens in beds and the fashion is for borders 'where an infinite variety of [flowers] are mingled together, but arranged so that they may blend one with another in colour as well as stature...'. He explains that the flowers should be staked if necessary and well spaced out from each other to show off each type. He also lists many and varied flowering shrubs ranging from the splendid *Magnolia grandiflora* to *Daphne cneorum* which Cobbett says is not fit for much but the front of borders and rock work.

In the list of work to be done in the flower garden in March, Cobbett tells his

readers to sow seeds of adonis, alyssum, prince's feather, snapdragon, yellow balsam, candytuft, catchfly, convolvulus minor (a great favourite of the flower painters), devil-in-a-bush, hawkweed, Indian pink, larkspurs, lavatera, linaria, mignonette, moonwort, nasturtiums, nigella, palma christi, pansy, sweet pea, persicaria, scabious, sunflowers, strawberry spinage, ten-week stocks, sweet sultan, venus-navel-wort. This a long list by any gardener's standards today, probably because it is no longer particularly popular or fashionable to grow annual flowers. The list continues of flowers to grow over heat from a hot bed such as zinnia, marvel-of-Peru, amaranthus and asters and Cobbett suggests planting bulbs for autumn flowering. Potted plants he advises should be carefully hardened off outdoors but the best tulips, hyacinths and auriculas should be protected from the worst weather. Cuttings should be taken from pinks and carnations to increase and renew old stock and path edgings of box, thrift or little clumps of daisies could be planted.

The use of hot beds and glass for bringing plants on faster and giving them winter protection was by then a highly advanced technique. Hot beds were an obvious device, given that horse and cow manure abounded, and meant that tender flowers could be grown and fruits and vegetables such as melons and cucumbers were no problem to crop in quantity. Cobbett explains how to start half-hardy flowers off under glass over slight heat and gives ideas for flowers to decorate the glasshouses during the summer when geraniums, myrtles and other non-winter hardy plants are moved outside for their summer sojourn leaving the glasshouse free for different and more exotic subjects. Large houses with space and plenty of staff would have been able to follow Cobbett's suggestions, but it is doubtful whether the average cottager would have afforded or used glass as a protection. He would probably, however, have made full use of manure to make a hot bed or two in which to grow choice and early vegetables and might have tried

•◆•

BELOW The mallow family inlcudes many varieties of good-natured and easy-going plants which, while they are not sophisticated, really pay for their keep in the garden, flowering over a very long period of time. The annual types make excellent cut flowers, although the delicacy of their petals belies this fact. There are small herbaceous types and also larger bush mallows which billow out from a border or shrubbery in a cloud of pink blossom.

ABOVE The bold scarlet, papery petals of the perennial oriental poppy are a brief clash of colour during late spring and early summer. Easy to grow and relishing clay or heavy soil, they tend to last for many years if left undisturbed. Children are fascinated by the black blotches inside the petals and the velvety purple-black pepper-pot centre and long stamens. There are many newer varieties in more subtle colours, including a pale salmon pink, a dusky grey pink and pure white.

LEFT A packed and productive corner of a kitchen garden has flowers, vegetables, and fruit scrambling in muddled profusion. Vegetable marrows are grown over an arch instead of on the flat which is more common, and sweet peas join them in a race up to the light. During this period the kitchen garden was a very important part of any good-sized estate. Run by an army of gardeners, it thrived on the very available horse manure and made use of the newer technology of growing under glass.

LEFT A brilliant combination of orange tulips with shaded purple and mauve violas is a stunning sight on a sunny spring morning. The range of tulips to choose from is now excellent, with types which will flower from March through to early June. They demand a lot of work if you lift them after flowering and store until the next year, but you can leave them in the ground and let them take their chance. Many types continue to flower year after year, but some will dwindle.

a few of the interesting and non-native tender flowers which were increasing in popularity. Amateur gardeners at that time would have been thrifty and careful, saving seed from one year to the next and increasing plant stocks by taking cuttings and splitting plants as they became large enough.

The increased reliability of heating glasshouses meant that it was possible to keep such tender plants as orchids through a northern winter and these were now beginning to be cultivated commercially. The large nurseries of the day were enormously successful and profitable, riding on the crest of a wave of new plant introductions and even employing their own collectors to search out new varieties of plants to add to their lists. One very important plant introduced in this period was the fuchsia. There are two stories of how it was brought into cultivation. One was that in 1788 a Captain Firth brought a plant to Kew Gardens, London, from where a nurseryman, James Lee, obtained a plant which he found easy to propagate. He only sold a few plants at a time, however, and kept the price artificially high. The second story suggests that Lee saw a fuchsia plant growing in the window of a small house in Wapping, Essex. The fuchsia had been a present from a sailor, home from abroad, to his wife. Lee persuaded the woman to part with the plant for eight guineas and he managed to raise about 300 cuttings from it, making a handsome profit on the transaction.

The Flower Contained

T he Georgian period spanned a very wide range of interior styles and fashions for furnishings and decorations. It saw a peak of perfection in cabinet-making skills and the exquisite fabrics and porcelain which were made to complement the fine furniture. Styles ranged from severe simplicity to the overblown rococo splendours of French furniture and interior architecture. A mixture of classic and gothic ideals was further complicated by Chinese and Indian influence which permeated the decorative arts in particular.

The understated and elegant quiet style of Robert Adam with his use of subtle colours, perfect proportions and superb craftsmanship was combined very often with the most lavish use of decoration, rich paintings and elaborate detailing in fabrics, curtains and drapes. An excellent example of this eclectic and ostentatious taste is the Royal Pavilion in Brighton, where the interiors reflect every influence

RIGHT This style of flower painting, which was so familiar during this period, found its way onto other materials apart from canvas. This detail is from a large and magnificent vase, glazed a deep lapis blue and generously decorated with gold and cream for contrast. Probably designed carefully to fit into a well-planned interior, a vase of this kind with its lid and ring handles was never intended as a container for flowers. The decorated panel shows roses, hollyhocks, poppies, honeysuckle and convolvulus.

Baskets were used as decorative flower containers because they were light and rustic with none of the heaviness of fussy ceramic vases. A swinging flower-filled basket was a common motif for porcelain and fabric, always decorated with twisty curving silk ribbons in the French style. Here, summer garden roses spill out of an antique-handled basket in an uninhibited mixture of colours. During the eighteenth century, strong pastel shades were very popular, often used with plenty of white to keep the theme fresh and airy. Before filling a basket, line it with damp flower foam. Use several different coloured roses of an old-fashioned and full-petalled type, if possible. Fill in with soft, mauvy-blue scabious and a few clematis, and try to include a stem or two of the deep blue convolvulus which so often appeared in eighteenth-century paintings.

LEFT A magnificent and imposing arrangement of summer flowers in the style of an eighteenth-century flower painting. There is no chosen colour scheme but rather a use of as many different types of flowers as possible, particularly garden flowers and foliage. A heavy garden composite urn is packed with damp florist's foam, and a piece of crumpled wire over the top of the foam helps to hold heavy or thick stems in place. To create this arrangement, which is designed to be seen from the front, begin by blocking in the outline with the tallest flowers. Gradually fill in, mixing colours and shapes more or less at random and using any short-stemmed blooms for the lower front of the urn. When you finally put the arrangement in position, bear in mind that it will look good seen from a slightly lower viewpoint than you might normally use.

RIGHT By this time the flower piece painting had become a stylized and beautiful decoration in its own right. The way in which the flowers were laid out and the choice of extra objects and natural history specimens seemed to follow a standard formula. A real or faux marble ledge was a very common surface for the vase and something was usually placed beside the flowers to add weight visually to a shape which would otherwise be top heavy. In this painting by Johan Laurentz Jensen a clutch of ripe cherries adds to the feeling of perfection created by the flowers. Each bloom is shown in sharp detail and is in exquisite condition – real flowers would find it hard to compete.

of the period and particularly those from the Far East.

The lightness and elegance laced with frivolity of this period meant that, as always, the floral motif was strongly in evidence. Around 1730 wallpaper in large flat sheets began to be quite widely used. Handpainted on heavy paper, wallpaper designs were mostly of flowers and foliage, trees and birds, owing much to Chinese influence.

This was also the time for chintz fabrics, which often combined stripes with posies or scattered flowers and swirling ribbons and bows. There was a freshness to these designs with their clean and clear colours, often pastels but quite strong. These pretty colours, used with large areas of white, made wonderfully romantic and elegant fabrics which were used generously in lavish window treatments, drapes and bed hangings. This was in great contrast to earlier periods when fabrics had been richly heavy and dense, often encrusted with embroidery and dyed in deep dark colours. By 1830 or so chintz fabrics were produced in quantity by machine, using very crude chemical dyes which in many cases spoiled the high quality of design and fine draughtsmanship.

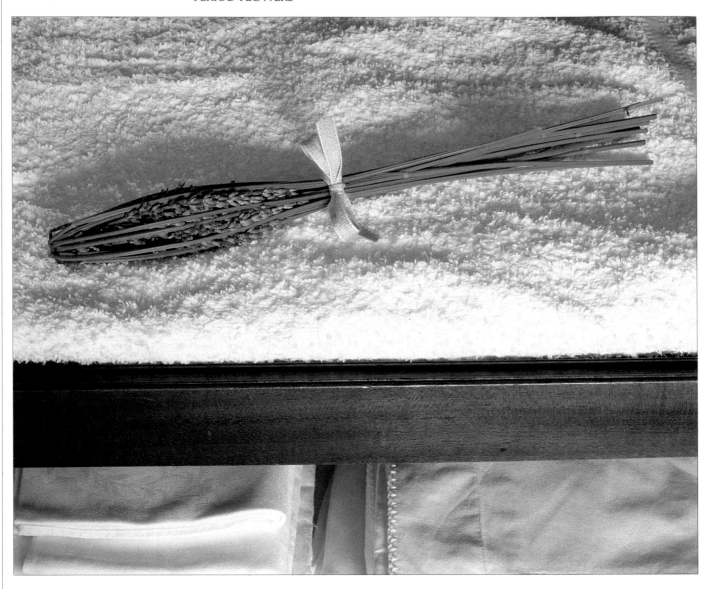

ABOVE A method of containing the small lavender bracts, which are prone to dropping off the stem amongst the linen, is to make lavender bottles. Use long-stemmed fresh lavender and allow it to dry naturally. Make a bunch of about 12 to 18 long stems and tie tightly with thin string just below the flowers. Working in order with one stem at a time, bend each stem right back on itself, enclosing the flowers. When all the stems are folded back, tie them in place to make a cage round the flowers. You can use a decorative ribbon for this. More elaborate bottles have narrow ribbon interlaced through the cage, but this can look over-fussy and hides the colour of the lavender.

RIGHT The use of herbs and flowers to scent and protect household linens continued through this period. City dwellers who could not grow their own plants were able to buy bunches of herbs and particularly lavender from street-sellers and market stalls. This little dried bunch makes use of lavender and hyssop to provide the scent and stems of southernwood to protect from clothes moth. The dried garden roses simply add their own scent and some colour and prettiness. Bind the stems of the bunch tightly with a rubber band or wire, as the stems go on shrinking after they are picked and dried. Cover this with a ribbon or tape bow, and hang the bunch from a hook or key.

RIGHT *Iris sibirica* is native to much of Europe, despite its Latin name, and it has been grown in gardens since Elizabethan times. The flowers are held on tall slender stems which gives the whole plant a pleasing delicate look, although it is tough and easy to grow. It can be grown beside water, but is just as happy in ordinary garden soil which does not contain too much lime. All the iris types make good flowers for picking and using in arrangements.

LEFT An eighteenth-century walnut chest-of-drawers makes the setting for a sophisticated arrangement of strongly-coloured flowers. The blooms have been chosen individually for their shapes and colours rather than to harmonize or make a complete colour scheme. The flowers echo the design which appears in the vase, so that there are fat full roses and small twining stems of nasturtiums and clematis combining to make a very pretty and romantic collection for a bedroom. In addition, the garden roses and sweet peas provide plenty of fragrance.

Flowers were used throughout living rooms and bedrooms as decorations. They were sometimes fresh, but artificial blooms, made from many materials ranging from silk, wax, paper or shells, were also used. Containers for all these arrangements began to be produced in larger quantities and factories such as those owned by the Wedgwood company made vases specifically for flowers. The new fashion of putting a mantelpiece around a fireplace demanded vases to fit and special pots were made to stand in the hearth where they would be filled with flowers during the summer months. Plants and evergreens would have been brought in from the garden and glasshouse to decorate, in a more formal way, the hall and the study. Many paintings and porcelain decorations at this time show elegant baskets filled with tumbling flowers swinging from silk ribbons. Ribbons were immensely popular both as decorations and to tie back fabric or hang prints and pictures. They echoed the curving and free shapes and lines beloved of this time. Dressing tables were invariably flower-decked with arrangements stood in front of a mirror to double the effect. One popular shape of vase was made up from a cluster of trumpet-shaped tubes to separate individual flowers and the hyacinth or bulb glass was commonly used to display spring-flowering bulbs. Large vases were often stood on matching or complementary stands and pillars to allow positioning for greatest effect. As dining became less a masculine enjoyment and mixed parties and dinners were becoming fashionable, the dining table became another focal point for floral decorations. Flowers, fruits and sweetmeats were often combined as an arrangement with moss and grass tucked in amongst them.

Flowers were used extensively to decorate women's hats and hair and were worn pinned to bodices and shoulders. Men too wore buttonholes and in portrait paintings of this period flowers are often seen as an accessory, either held in the hand or lying nearby, as well as inserted amongst elaborately dressed curls of hair or to embellish a lace-edged décolletage.

CHAPTER FIVE

A
FLORAL INSPIRATION
THE VICTORIAN VIEW

The Victorian age saw further developments in the collecting and breeding of new plants in Britain. The British Empire stretched wide and far across the world and the confidence of the horticultural sciences was no less than that of every other branch of science and of commerce and trade, industry and learning. The Industrial Revolution brought profound changes to the landscape and to the lives of ordinary people who rushed to the cities. But a large population of rural workers was still needed, and even in the towns, apart from the grimy back-to-back dwellings and crowded terraces of cheap and poor-quality housing, most people with a house of their own had some kind of garden in which to grow a few flowers or produce.

The large country house was still a very desirable asset for the rich, and the many industrialists and businessmen made newly wealthy by the success and expansion of Victoria's reign were quick to commission vast mansions complete with large-scale pleasure grounds and productive kitchen gardens. A whole range of plants never seen before in this country was introduced and certain varieties became highly fashionable. The Victorians' love of order, discipline and control re-instated a more formal style of gardening while their desire for the exotic and unusual threatened to swamp the view with enormous conifers, tropical palms and weirdly-shaped monkey puzzle trees. Colours were brash and bold, detailing was intricate, and mechanical devices and inventions were curious and clever, culminating in an unprecedented display of exuberance and confidence.

A posy of sky-blue forget-me-nots makes a perfect Victorian Valentine.

The Victorian Garden

LEFT Rhododendrons and azaleas were responsible for some of the greatest changes in the look of the British garden. While new plants had been arriving in Britain for centuries, they generally fitted in with indigenous species and other established newcomers with little impact. Rhododendrons and azaleas, by their scale and colour range, could not be ignored and they were often planted to cover large areas of land in Victorian times. Since they require conditions of woodland and acid soil, they can only be grown in certain parts of Britain. Here, at the Lea rhododendron gardens near Matlock in Derbyshire, a winding path leads through splendid specimens of rhododendrons which in this area of the garden are in soft colours of pink, cream and white.

The eighteenth-century school of landscape gardening had been largely abandoned and, under the influence of designers such as Humphrey Repton, the flower garden was restored near to the house and the art of gardening was reinstated according to historical precedent. The garden was perceived as a work of art and it was no longer considered right that any deception should take place in the form of fake countryside, 'natural' woodland or romantic vistas. However, the emphasis on designing a garden which was imaginative led to much confusion as to what was acceptable, resulting in some extraordinarily lavish gardens which seemed to include every style there was at the time. Terms such as picturesque, architectural, French, Italianate, rustic and geometric were all invented to describe the layout and plantings of fashionable gardens of the day.

All these ideas reinforced the mood which presumed that order and control were all important. There was still enough cheap labour, as well as some mechanization of garden tasks, to make and maintain gardens of the highest quality and grandest ideals. Rockeries could be larger, grass finer, plants more exotic, seasonal fruits and vegetables earlier, and flower beds more colourful and intricate, than ever before.

Row upon row of neat suburban villas each had their small front garden and plot of land at the back. A general style of gardening soon emerged for these, based more on ideas from the grand estate than from the country cottage. Rural gardens on the whole remained unchanged but the growing middle classes liked a front garden which looked like a bedding scheme from one of the many new municipal parks and pleasure gardens. As the passion for newly imported plants such as rhododendrons and azaleas grew, so did the desire to build gardens on acid soil which would support them. Suddenly parts of the country which had never been chosen before for creating large gardens became desirable, so that expanses of Hampshire and Surrey, Staffordshire and Yorkshire became home to swathes of alien shrubs and trees, looking like outcrops of the Himalayas or North America.

One such grand Victorian garden was created at Biddulph Grange in Staffordshire and plans of it show a huge area of annexed land virtually cut off from the surrounding countryside in its own private domain. There was of course a large house and offices, a stable yard and terraces, glasshouses for tender rhododendrons and camellias and an orangery. There were plantations of mixed trees, a pinetum and arboretum and one avenue of limes and another of Wellingtonia. There was a Chinese garden, a rhododendron garden, many water gardens and a bowling green and quoit ground. There was a whole walk devoted to dahlias, a ferny dell with a stream running through it, an Egyptian court made of clipped yew and statuary, and miles of walks and pathways from which to enjoy the whole layout. Planned in 1842 it was very much a garden of the period, containing all the newly popular plants and devices at the height of fashion. Today the garden sounds sombre, heavy and over complicated, set as it was amid a piece of bleak swampy moorland. The owner of the house was in fact a passionately keen gardener and his particular subject was orchids. Many of the great gardens of this period were laid out and planted by knowledgeable and enthusiastic amateur or professional horticulturalists who were also able to afford such grand schemes.

The Victorians were responsible for the planting of many evergreen trees not previously grown in Britain. The few indigenous species were no match for the new ranks of colossal giants soon to begin their march across the countryside. Their neat outlines and rich sombre greens, which of course remained through every season, captured the Victorian imagination and soon no garden worth anything could afford not to have a specimen or two of some foreign evergreen standing guard beside the shrubbery.

The removal of tax on sheet glass in 1845 meant that there was an upsurge in the building of glasshouses and conservatories, which neatly coincided with the interest in growing and collecting tender plants and tropical species. Coal and coke for heating systems were cheap and plentiful and old-fashioned hot-bed methods were still used. It was not unusual for large estate kitchen gardens to have row upon row of glasshouses along an inside wall devoted to individual plants such as

ABOVE The common camellia, a native of Japan and Korea, was introduced in 1739 to Great Britain and was soon followed by many more cultivars from China and Japan. Requiring similar conditions to rhododendrons and azaleas, camellias were a great status symbol for the Victorian gardener. The perfect blooms damage easily but make beautiful decorations and were often pinned into elaborately dressed hair for balls and parties.

cucumbers, melons, figs, grapes, peaches, orchids, pelargoniums, gardenias, camellias, house plants and pineapples. Joseph Paxton, gardener to the Duke of Devonshire at Chatsworth, designed and built there one of the greatest glasshouses or conservatories of the day. It covered an acre of land and reached 67 feet off the ground at the ridge of the roof. In 1849 at Chatsworth, Paxton succeeded in the flowering of the giant water-lily, *Victoria amazonica*, which had leaves big enough to support a child's weight. He built a special glasshouse big enough to contain the large areas of water needed to grow the water-lily and from this design he went on to plan and construct the largest glasshouse ever built, the one which housed the Great Exhibition of 1851 in London. Another great glass construction had been built at Kew gardens between 1844 and 1848. Known as the Palm House and designed by Decimus Burton and Richard Turner, it was a massive structure built on curving shapes and ample enough to contain the growing collection of tropical plants of the Royal Botanic Garden.

It is an oversimplification to say that the flower garden returned to a formal arrangement of plants laid out in rows and colour patterns within a carefully prescribed shape. In fact, the garden moved through many phases during this period but the strongest image which remains is the kind of summer bedding schemes still used in seasonal resorts and certain town parks. Spikey sub-tropical foliage is surrounded by rings or lines of brilliant annuals occasionally toned down by a little grey foliage. Done well this kind of gardening can be quite breathtaking, but translated into a small suburban plot it often looks garish and artificial. By 1845 it was becoming common practice to fill beds with exotics and tender flowers, which were now being more cheaply produced in greater quantities. There were already warnings about combining the right colours and in an edition of *Floral World* the editor felt impelled to say 'If you look around the gardens just now, you

BELOW Ornamental cherry trees became very popular during the Victorian period with new varieties being introduced all the time from Japan, China, Korea and the Himalayas. At this time there were already many types to choose from, as they had been brought to Britain from North America and elsewhere over many centuries. Cherries were planted in suburban gardens and on large country estates, and the relative dullness of the tree except when it is briefly in flower did not seem to undermine its popularity. Short-lived and prone to disease, the cherry is still widely planted for its spectacular display of blossom in spring, and anyone who has stood beneath the branches of a fully-laden flowering cherry on a sunny blue-skied day never forgets the sight.

LEFT The double herbaceous border on a grand scale can still be seen today, although few houses can employ as many gardeners as in Victorian times. This superb example at Benington Lordship garden in Hertfordshire, however, has all the extravagance and style of the nineteenth century. The colours are strong and bold but there is a slight informality in the way the lower plants at the front of the border spill out and over the gravel walk.

will see many examples of geraniums and calceolarias in juxtaposition . . . but the effect is a vulgar glare of colour which tires the eye and gives no pleasure to cultivated taste.' People were advised to plant contrasting colours together such as red and green, blue and yellow, dark blue with orange yellow, and greenish yellow with violet. Non-complementary colours were thought to be improved by the addition of white plants. As the fashion for bedding-out schemes continued, so new and better plants were introduced, together with a much larger range of foliage plants. These proved very satisfactory during poor summers when flowers did not do well. Dwarf and small varieties of plants were used to produce the effect called carpet bedding, which was as near to the Tudor idea of pattern-filled parterres as was possible. Of course all the larger flowers on taller stems were still grown as cut flowers, particularly in large gardens where it was possible to provide space for growing blooms just to be cut for the house. As we shall see, there were changes to the style of floral decoration indoors which echoed exactly what was happening in the flower garden outside.

In previous centuries the garden had been a place for recreation as well as inspiration and the Victorian age was no different. There would be areas of perfectly kept close-cut lawn for bowls, croquet, tennis and other games; walks and

BELOW The familiar mop-headed or Hortensia hydrangeas are mostly hybrids bred from the late nineteenth- and early twentieth-century introductions from China, Japan, Korea and the United States of America. They make useful late summer flowering shrubs and the mop-head versions are excellent, as even after flowering the shrub takes on lovely autumn colours and looks good well into the winter. The flower heads of some varieties change to delicious subtle colours of bronze, pink, green and blue and can be picked and dried for winter arrangements.

diversions for those who just wanted to stroll and talk; summer houses, pergolas and arbours in which to linger, make meetings, take tea or paint a watercolour. The interest in the so-called rustic style resulted in the building of many quaint and peculiar little buildings. Unstripped poles and branches were constructed into arches, summer houses and garden seats. Not a straight line was included and the roof might be thatched in straw or heather. Stone and cement work was sometimes decorated with shells and pebbles in a seaside version of the rustic, and the deck chair was moved from the ocean liner to the garden lawn and verandah. Cast iron, which at this time was being used in ever more creative and clever ways, found itself in the garden as seating and tables, as well as in much of the important structure and mechanisms for the glasshouses and conservatories.

Flowers of the Period

LEFT Pansies and violas of all kinds seem very happy grown in containers and pots. Many plants resent the restriction of such conditions and never do their best, but pansies thrive with only a little help. They will need regular watering and the occasional liquid feed, and if they appear to be getting leggy and sprawling, then shear them over and wait for another crop of flowers to start again. There are winter-flowering varieties now which will flower through all but the iciest spells, and for the summer months plants can be grown from seed or bought as small plants, or named varieties can be chosen from specialist nurseries.

•❦•

•❦•

RIGHT *Convallaria majalis* or lily of the valley was also sometimes known as the wood lily or the May lily. In ancient times the flowers were distilled to make *aqua aurea* and kept in vessels of gold. There was a belief that the flower distilled with wine could restore lost speech or memory. The lily of the valley grows wild in almost all parts of Europe and demands a moist soil and a shady position. In a garden, a bed at the foot of a north wall was the traditional place to grow these flowers. The Victorians adored the sweet scent and delicate construction of the plant, and lilies of the valley were often included in bouquets and posies. Pots of the roots or crowns were brought under cover and forced to flower during the winter to make exquisite table pieces and decorations for buffet tables. The fragrance was captured for perfumes and toilet waters and suited the Victorian style of quite heavy and sweet scents which also had a freshness and naturalness to them.

The range of flower types loved by the Victorians is extraordinarily wide, encompassing the most exotic, rare and difficult through to the very humble and ordinary. As with most things Victorian, this breadth reflected the enormous differences between the classes and the completely separate worlds that they inhabited. Many of the favourite flowers were those which had been recently discovered and brought back to Britain surrounded by mystique, which gave them great desirability. Others on the list, like the violet and pansy, had been popular for centuries but for some reason the Victorians seem almost to have re-invented them.

By 1840 many horticultural societies formed, holding meetings and annual shows, and there were several horticultural journals available to anyone who could afford them, exerting immense influence on what flowers people chose to grow. The favourite florist flowers of earlier times dwindled in popularity and some such as pinks, while still grown and shown extensively in the mid nineteenth century, were to decline within the next twenty years. During the decade 1830 to 1840 the dahlia gained rapid popularity as a florist flower and the chrysanthemum joined the list and was shown during the autumn. By the end of the century, shows were held which included vegetables and fruit alongside the chrysanthemums and dahlias but there seemed to be no classes left for the older choices of auricula and ranunculus.

The scented herbaceous peony was bred and developed at this time and many new and beautiful French varieties appeared. Their large and blowsy full-petalled shapes seem entirely suited to the age of the hoop petticoat and crinoline dress. Roses too remained a much-loved flower and growers were crossing and hybri-

A delicate pink, blue and white posy contains a mixture of scented flowers. The Victorians adored the tiny, white, fragrant bells of lily of the valley and forced roots into flower at all times of year to provide material for bouquets, table decorations and buttonholes. Normally in bloom at the end of May, lily of the valley is a plant which relishes a moist soil and some shade to produce its best flowers. Ferns were another Victorian passion and were used as pot plants, to decorate food and tables and as a delicate living frill to surround posies and bouquets. The starting point for this posy is a fat, scented rosebud ringed with deep blue hyacinth flowers. Next there are smaller, shell-pink roses and sprays of London Pride (*Saxifraga umbrosa*). Finally a ring of lily of the valley and a flourish of deep green leather-fern contain the whole posy neatly and sweetly.

LEFT A handful of cheerful violas light up an old barn window. The Scottish firm of nurserymen, Dicksons of Edinburgh, began in 1867 to improve the ordinary pansy in an attempt to produce a plant more suitable for bedding. At first these plants were known as tufted pansies but later came to be called violas. By combining the pollen of several viola species such as *Viola lutea, Viola cornuta* and *Viola grievii* with show and fancy pansies, James Grieve the breeder produced some important new varieties. As popular as ever, violas are hardy and long-flowering, making lovely informal patches of colour at the front of a border or contributing in a more formal way to a spring bedding scheme. This little bi-coloured viola is Jackanapes which has a small flower more like a *Viola cornuta* than many of the named violas. Violas come in white, cream, yellow, mauve and purple, and many are bi-coloured or with contrasting edges or streaks.

❦

RIGHT In one family of plants, the earlier liking for striped and feathered petals has remained to a small degree. The rose Ferdinand Pichard has quite small and neat blooms and each is striped with crimson on a white or very pale pink ground. It is from the Bourbon family of roses which were the predecessors of the modern Hybrid Teas and, although they have the old-fashioned leaves and flowers of the earlier roses, they have the advantage of perpetual flowering.

dizing many of the current varieties to produce yet more new forms and colorations. The rose was important enough to warrant a special area of garden or at least separate beds for its cultivation and many clever constructions were devised to train climbing and rambling types along and over.

The Victorians seem to have loved bell-shaped flowers such as lily of the valley which was grown in large patches against north walls and in shady borders and shrubberies. In large gardens, the roots were dug up during the winter months, potted into elaborate shapes or table centrepieces, and forced with heat to flower much earlier than they might normally.

Rhododendrons, camellias and azaleas were three of the most sought after and popular flowers of the period. They were essentially garden flowers to be seen in vibrant masses grown through woodland and under tall specimen trees. No doubt those who owned gardens filled with these plants cut some branches for house decoration, and camellias were certainly often used for hair decorations, corsages and buttonholes. Pots containing dwarf varieties of these shrubs were grown under glass and brought indoors during winter months to decorate rooms.

Violets, pansies and violas were taken up with great interest by the Victorian plant breeders. The pansy for a time was very much a florist flower, but it was not until the very end of the nineteenth century that the first violas and violettas were raised by crossing pansies with the native *Viola lutea* of the mountain grasslands of northern Britain. Violets were a Victorian flower of fashion and at Windsor three thousand plants were grown under glass frames to supply the royal household through the winter with bunches of fresh flowers. Baskets of violets for sale were a common sight on city street corners, each little posy encircled with violet or ivy leaves and tied with thread. City clerks often wore a bunch as a buttonhole. Although there was a thriving British industry growing sweet violets for cutting, it could not compare with the south of France where some 13,000 lbs of blooms were harvested each year for the flower trade.

The rose was a source of inspiration for patterns and decorations and appeared on china, wallpapers, dress fabrics and furnishings. It was usually depicted as a large old-fashioned cabbage rose with more than a hint of the rococo style about it. Not until the arts and crafts movement and under the influence of designers such as A. F. Vigers, William Morris, C. F. A. Voysey and Bruce Talbert, did the fashion for simple flowers, and wild roses in particular, begin to appear and the taste for elaborate and romantic flowers begin to wane. These little paper napkin rings are copies of Victorian paper printing, depicting pink and white roses with blue convolvulus. It is possible to buy these but the idea could easily be copied using strips of wallpaper border, or by drawing and painting your own design taken from an original fabric or piece of china.

The Victorian Interior

After the feeling of lightness and space of the Georgian age there came a great change through the Victorian period in the furniture and decoration of house interiors. From simplicity and elegance there developed a feel for richness, opulence and detail which threatened to smother every home, whether grand or ordinary, in a layer of extraneous clutter. This was the time when every table had to be covered with at least two cloths and windows were draped and swathed in yards of fabric. Shelves were edged, lamps were shaded, chairs were protected by antimacassars and furniture legs were covered for modesty's sake. Velvet and

LEFT Children and scenes of childhood were favourite subjects for Victorian painters. In this painting by Charles Trevor Garland a blonde-haired, blue-eyed, rosy-cheeked little girl diffidently offers an outsize posy of roses. There was an elaborate language of flowers at this time which many people used when giving flowers or flower-decorated cards. Roses invariably spelt out love and constancy.

ABOVE Sentimentality knew no bounds in Victorian times and when messages of love and affection were difficult to convey in person, then elaborate cards took the place of the spoken word. Here is a present-day collection of Victorian Valentine's Day cards, which include forget-me-nots, roses, lily of the valley and violets as part of their messages which always involved the use of flowers.

chenille were favourite fabrics; walls were papered with elaborate designs; pictures and prints began to be used merely as decoration and wall fillers; no space was left unfilled which could be crammed with china ornaments, knick-knacks or souvenirs. Furniture was plump and comfortable looking but usually overstuffed, hard and unyielding, but then a straight back and an upright deportment were attitudes to be cultivated and admired.

Much use was made of flowers throughout the house, though it seemed possible that the house plant might usurp the flower's position as prime decoration for parlour or hall. A household wealthy enough to maintain a staff of gardeners and a kitchen garden might expect flowers cut and delivered every day. Very often these were arranged by the head gardener once he had been given orders as to what was needed. As well as arrangements for dining rooms and sitting rooms, flowers might

The tradition of the hand-held posy continued into Victorian times without any waning of its popularity. Posies were used as gifts and decorations and the style during this period was for neat and organized rings of colour made up from different varieties of flowers and leaves. The idea is simple and quick to copy and is still one of the best ways to turn a few flowers into a welcome present. Once the pleasure of receiving it is over, it can be enjoyed for several more days by simply standing the whole thing in water in a small container where it becomes a ready-made flower arrangement. Begin by choosing one central flower such as a rose or something quite solid and with substance. Make a ring of different flowers round the rose and then, working outwards, continue to make rings of flowers finishing with a frill of leaves or, as here, something light and airy such as these *Alchemilla mollis* flower heads. You could make a posy using only roses in different colours or choosing one colour of flower separated by contrasting leaves. The small posy here is made from yellow rose buds, golden marjoram, lavender, violas and alchemilla. The Victorians often used these little nosegays to spell out a message through the use of specific flowers. Tie or wire the stems tightly to keep everything in place and cut the stems off evenly at the bottom to look neat. A pretty bow and ribbon is an optional extra. A posy of this kind, made for a bridal bouquet, would usually have all the flower stems wired individually to keep the flowers very neat and organized.

LEFT With the abundance of cheap coal to heat glasshouses and highly sophisticated structures designed for the purpose, a Victorian gentleman could indulge a passion for growing orchids. These plants had exactly the right cachet for the fashionable collector as they were expensive, exotic and required skill and special treatment to do well. Pots of flowering orchids were brought indoors to grace drawing rooms and halls, or they might have filled a conservatory where they could be enjoyed by the family and shown off to friends and guests. There are several varieties which can be grown in the house and do not demand imitation tropical conditions.

be required for buttonholes or for dressing ladies' hair for dances and dinner parties. Cold and wet weather would not be expected to interrupt the supply of blooms so a heated glasshouse would be kept functioning, providing scented and exotic flowers such as stephanotis, orange blossom, gardenias and camellias as well as plants of orchids, schizanthus, lilies, cyclamen, gesneras, azaleas, primulas, cinerarias and dozens of other varieties of showy and colourful flowering plants.

In more modest households run on a few staff, the lady or daughter of the house might reasonably expect to arrange the flowers as a suitable and creative pastime. Jugs and vases of mixed garden flowers were most frequently used and the fashion for dotting things around in a room meant that several pieces of furniture might be decorated with separate floral arrangements. Alongside the fresh flowers there would often be vases of dried flowers and seedheads and – a great Victorian favourite – grasses. Wax flowers and fabric flowers were also used and these were sometimes stood beneath large clear glass domes to keep the arrangements safe and dustfree. The fashion for ferns extended indoors and pots of maidenhair and asparagus fern seemed able to survive the often gloomy and stuffy conditions perfectly well. Many other foliage plants were used also, including palms, caladiums and aspidistras, and were made more decorative by being stood in a fine cache-pot or urn and placed in state on a tall plant stand or special pillar.

BELOW This double arrangement of full-blown garden roses and mixed annual poppies has more than a hint of the influence of Fantin Latour, who painted richly beautiful flower paintings. Latour often used roses as a subject, frequently in baskets rather than in formal vases. Here the roses are supported in damp foam inside a lined shallow basket, while the poppies stand in a modern simple clear glass vase. Shirley poppies and the peony-flowered opium poppies are short-lived, but will last for two or three days in water if the ends of their stems are first seared over a flame or stood in boiling water for a few seconds. Varieties of the opium poppy were bred from the seventeenth century but it was not until the 1880s that the Reverend W Wilks from Shirley, in Surrey, improved varieties of the field poppy (*Papaver rhoeas*) to produce an amazing range of sherbet and icecream-coloured single and double poppies.

All the well-known pottery manufacturers of the day produced several ranges of jardinières and Chinese pots to house this jungle of greenery. Even if there was a conservatory attached to one of the living rooms, designed to be visited and perhaps used as an extra room, space would still be made in other parts of the house for plants and flowers. For those whose rooms suffered from a lack of fresh air due to gas fittings, the Wardian case provided the answer. This device looked like a miniature glasshouse which was stood near a window and nurtured the green plants inside in a more suitable atmosphere than the surrounding room could offer.

There was a great vogue at this time for practical, 'how-to' books, hence the many titles on garden creation, cooking and household management. There was a general preoccupation with being seen to do the right thing and when it came to arranging flowers, particularly for the dining table, it was possible to buy books containing elaborate diagrams and instructions for floral fantasies, designed to impress your dinner-party guests. The Georgian and early Victorian dinner table was laid with everything required for the whole meal and no space was left for flowers or decorations, but by 1850 it became fashionable to dine *à la Russe*, with each course served from the sideboard by a servant. This meant that the table could now be filled with flowers and for the next thirty years or so this new floral art form reached fabulous heights. Swags of twining smilax were draped and tented over the diners and looped along the table edge. Tall glass stands and épergnes were filled with mixtures of ferns, grasses and flowers and often fruit was added too. Colour was carefully controlled, avoiding yellows which looked poor in artificial light and using much red, white and pink, always set off by plenty of green foliage. Much use was made of moss and ivy to conceal the mechanics of all this and room was left for candelabra and silver to add glitter and sparkle, either on a highly polished surface or a snow-white damask cloth.

This large-scale basket arrangement of late summer flowers contains many of the rich and dense tones which the Victorians used in their fabrics and interiors. While this style of closely-packed blooms is often used now, a hundred years ago the preference was for sparser arrangements with more space around each flower, although the extravagance and scale of this design would probably have appealed to Victorian tastes. Choose a strong basket and after lining it carefully to avoid water leaking out, pack it with florist foam to hold all the stems. Decide where the finished basket is to stand before putting the first pieces in place. Only when you know if the arrangement will be seen from all views, or from above, or from one side only, can you work out an outline shape and eye-level. If possible work at the same height and position as the finished basket will stand and aim for a gentle mix of shades of colour without any very jumpy contrasts between flowers. Here the solid blooms of carnations, roses, echinops and lilies are off-set by lighter-weight, smaller-scale fillers such as michaelmas daisy, statice and polygonum.

The Cottage Window

Rural cottages with their small windows and lack of light inside did not make good homes for flowers or plants, but in Victorian times every windowsill would have had its row of bright geraniums, begonias or calceolarias. They made a cheerful screen through which to watch the world go by and the tough old plants seemed to thrive in their limited space. A few cut flowers from an allotment or front garden would have been picked regularly for the mantelpiece or sideboard and the winter months might have been cheered with a vase of silvery honesty seedheads or bright, dried flowers. Everyone would have had their favourite flowers for picking and there was always a choice from the fields and woods too. But what had been plentiful in the wild began to come under threat as the new mobility brought by the railways meant that special country excursions were arranged for city dwellers to pick wild daffodils. There were plenty of hidden places, however, where trains and roads did not yet reach and those who chose to could still pick bushels of cowslips or primroses to make cowslip wine, a country favourite since medieval days.

In country homes flowers were still used for other purposes such as the making of medicines or cough mixtures, hair rinses and flavourings for syrups, drinks and puddings. Recipes made use of abundant wild flowers, such as elderflowers, to make simple but delicious dishes like pancakes and fritters. Flowers and leaves from the garden made cheap alternatives to expensive tea and coffee and even now, in Europe, tisanes and drinks such as camomile and lime-blossom infusions are widely made and drunk at home.

RIGHT Pelargoniums were a great garden and greenhouse favourite for the Victorians. Seen in every cottage window or grand manor house bedding scheme, the cheerful, brilliant, single red blooms are the essence of simplicity and evoke summer like no other flower. Choose the old-fashioned types to grow if you want to be authentic. Many of the modern hybrids have been bred with over-large flower heads which seem out of scale to the plant, producing a top-heavy look combined with crude colour. The single reds, such as Gustav Emich, and all the varieties known as the Uniques have the old-fashioned look about them and many of the ornamental and variegated leaf cultivars have great charm when used sympathetically. Here a group of three different varieties makes a brilliant still life sitting on top of an old oak water butt. To get the real Beatrix Potter feel of the potting shed in Mr MacGregor's garden, you will need to plant your pelargoniums into terracotta pots, not plastic ones.

LEFT In this painting by Eugene Claude, the casual arrangement of white and mauve lilacs in a basket appears to suggest that the branches have just been gathered and will shortly be taken inside to fill vases in the house. Lilac has long been a popular cut flower, lasting well in water, and today it is still grown commercially and forced into early bloom for sale during late winter months when few shrub flowers are available. Always hammer or split woody stems before arranging them so that they take up the maximum amount of water possible from the container. Stripping off the leaves along the stem will also prolong the life of the flowers.

CHAPTER SIX

GRAND THEMES
AND
FLORAL FASHIONS
THE EDWARDIAN ERA

This short period of twenty years or so from the last few years of Victoria's reign to the beginning of the First World War combined the excesses and successes of the previous half century with a definite feeling of change in the air as a new century began. The brief Edwardian period has often been described as one long garden party of tea on the lawn, cricket and croquet, and dances and parties after dark. The landscape was enjoying the last few years before the car brought a wholesale change, and farming, though by now quite highly mechanized, still worked at a pace governed by a man and his horse. There was an increase in the building of middle-sized and middle-class houses or villas, often on the edges of small towns or large villages, and where there was already a 'big' house in the village it was very much the focus for people in an almost feudal way.

The Empire and beyond still provided a challenge for plant collectors. China, India and Tibet all offered up wonderful new flower treasures for British and European gardeners, and the great and successful nurseries of the day continued to thrive. While the search for new plants continued, some of the old favourites were worked on and developed, often by amateurs or small nurserymen, and flowers such as the sweet pea, iris and day lily were lifted out of the shadows of the herbaceous border into the limelight of shows and competitions, and found a place in every colourful catalogue.

The art of garden design was brought into the lives of many more people than before. Where previously only hundreds of acres would have been worthy of the garden designers' time now they worked on small and average-sized gardens belonging to a much wider public.

The arts and crafts movement and a revival of interest in all things gothic and romantic brought with them a feeling for movement and fluidity in fashion, interiors and flowers. Space and lightness were to take over from the crowded and cluttered dimly lit Victorian room and the flowers of the period reflected this change.

The elegant waxy blooms of orchids, stephanotis and gardenia wait to adorn and scent an Edwardian evening.

The Edwardian Garden

—◆—

There were many important people during this period who had a profound influence on the way gardens were to look and the plants that they were to contain. Names such as Robinson, Jekyll, Willmott and Johnston are familiar still and some of their work remains today to provide us with a living link with the Edwardian period.

William Robinson was a prolific author of books about gardening and he owned and edited the magazine called *Gardening*, later to be changed to *Gardening Illustrated*. This publication was aimed very much at the new class of suburban dwellers who had enough time and money to spend on their modest gardens. A great influence on Robinson was the traditional cottage garden with its delicious jumble of flowers and vegetables, a clipped shrub or two, fruit trees and mixed hedges. In it he saw the wild flowers which he loved and collected, and a way of combining essentially incompatible plants into a harmonious presentation, deriving from a functional rather than a decorative purpose. He was to write a book entitled *The Wild Garden*, which was an entirely new concept for this period though much of his advice

RIGHT This deep and generous garden border, filled with hardy herbaceous plants in an uninhibited colour mix, is based on the idea of the filled-to-overflowing cottage garden but is tempered with some order and formality. It represents the Edwardian ideal of mixing shrubs and smaller plants together and using soft curves for the edges of borders. This style continues today and is used for both large and small gardens. It works well because it provides all-year-round colour and foliage interest and requires relatively little maintenance.

—◆—

LEFT Hidcote Manor Garden, which is now owned by the National Trust, is one of the handful of exceptional twentieth-century gardens created in Great Britain. Started by an American, Lawrence Johnston, early in the century, it was designed as a series of small gardens, to surround the existing Gloucestershire stone manor house. Each area of garden was devoted to one theme or idea and the planting by Johnston was highly original and inspired. Hidcote is now a must on the garden visitors' trail and the ideas it contains are still relevant and thought-provoking today.

LEFT Large old-fashioned pots filled with pelargoniums are useful for adding highlights of colour throughout the summer garden. The regal pelargoniums with their larger, more delicate flowers prefer to be in as sheltered a place as possible, and too much rain can damage their petals. An altogether tougher choice is the lovely Unique called Paton's Unique, whose single flowers are pink-blotched with a white throat.

⚫

BELOW A view of an Edwardian garden by William F. Ashburner shows a young woman picking summer flowers from a colourful herbaceous border. Her timeless dress and the pair of white doves give the painting a romantic feel but the flowers in their setting show a stylized version of the ideal Edwardian country cottage garden.

seems to have been on the placing of plants in sympathetic groupings. He appears to have despised the Victorian style of bedding out and carpet planting of tender summer flowers, yet he described quite elaborate schemes for flower beds, all the while trying to emphasize the importance of the plants over design for its own sake. Robinson is credited with having first thought of naturalizing daffodils and other bulbs in grass and growing them in patches and swathes as if they were wild. It was not really until the 1890s that daffodils were grown in sufficient quantities and at a price which made it possible to plant them in such profusion.

For a time William Robinson was joined on his magazine by Gertrude Jekyll, who was an artist until her sight began to fail and she took up garden design instead. She used her artist's sense of colour to design great billowing herbaceous borders, arranging plants in an unconventional and often sculptural way. She also wrote many books during her long life and it is considered that some of her finest garden plans were those on which she collaborated with the architect Edwin Lutyens. The colours she chose to use are very much what fashionable gardeners today strive to copy: soft blues, pinks, mauves and purples as well as white and cream were the usual palette. She loved using grey foliage plants as a foil for other colours and seems to have pre-empted the fashion for white and silver borders. In her large garden in Surrey she landscaped and planted a wood, making it into a series of pictures at every turn in the path – she was able to work on such a large scale because labour was still available and very cheap.

Another important female character with similar grand ideas was Ellen Willmott, who owned houses and gardens in Essex and France. A botanist and plant collector, she was also a garden designer of great taste and skill judging by

RIGHT Gertrude Jekyll and Edwin Lutyens combined their immense creativity in the design of the gardens at Hestercombe House in Somerset and recently, after years of obscurity, work has been done to restore the gardens to something of their former glory. This sturdy wooden and stone pergola at Hestercombe is very typical of the large-scale architectural features usually found in a Lutyens/Jekyll garden, while the planting and soft colour scheme is pure Gertrude Jekyll. Mounds of soft mauve lavender and yellow-flowered phlomis flourish in the dappled sunlight under pale pink climbing roses scrambling up the rustic stone pillars.

·❖·

ABOVE The hardy perennial catmint is a lovely plant to use to billow out from the front of a mixed border or to grow under beds of old-fashioned roses. The soft mauve flowers curve gracefully forward producing a lovely hazy cloud of colour. There are several varieties of different sizes to choose from, but all types are irresistible to some cats who, attracted by the scent, eat the new leaves in spring or flatten the plant by rolling on it. If you live in a cat-free neighbourhood, try growing it and pick some stems for indoor arrangements as it lasts well in water.

·❖·

LEFT This watercolour painting by Alfred Ernest Parsons depicts a corner of Ellen Willmott's magnificent garden at Warley End in Essex. She grew at least a hundred thousand species there, including her great interest – roses. The border here includes white and yellow lilies, artemesia, delphiniums and ceanothus, at the height of their beauty during July.

paintings of her garden at Warley Place in Essex. Her book *The Genus Rosa* had great influence in opening people's eyes to the many ramblers and species roses which tended to be overlooked amongst the big and blowsy confections of the rose breeders' lists. At one time at Warley Place, Ellen Willmott employed eighty-six gardeners to look after glasshouses, propagating houses, a three-acre rock garden, orchids and roses as well as herbaceous borders, wild areas and water and bog gardens. Sadly, by the thirties there was practically no trace of the garden, and such lavish garden projects were a thing of the past.

Another great gardener and plantsman working at this time was Edward Bowles who lived in an old family house in Enfield in London. Prevented by family circumstance from entering Holy Orders, he put his energy and time into creating a beautiful garden from the rather gloomy Victorian one he inherited, filling it with plants many of which he collected from Europe and North Africa. He had a long association with the Royal Horticultural Society and wrote many books about bulbs and about his own garden in which he worked for nearly ninety years.

Flowers of the Period

The Edwardians had many favourite flowers and improved versions of old varieties to choose from for their herbaceous borders. The exotics and tender species were as popular as in Victorian times, but there was a definite move outdoors to hardy perennials and annuals which provided a colourful backbone to an English summer garden. The dense and gloomy evergreen shrubberies of the previous century gave way to flowering shrubs and trees, and all the bulbs came into their own, grown in the more natural setting of woodland or rough grass rather than beds of bare earth.

There were great strides forward in the breeding of new varieties of daffodil, culminating in the production of the first pink-cupped white daffodil in 1923 named Mrs R O Backhouse after the wife of the man who bred it. Lilies were another species which had always been a popular garden and pot plant but which had not been worked on much by the plant breeders. With its medieval looks and connotations, the lily was often depicted by the pre-Raphaelite painters and was a highly fashionable flower of the period. It appeared as a motif in fabric and

RIGHT Dahlia plants did not reach England until 1798 and were not properly established until 1804 after it was realized that the tubers were not hardy in an average British winter and needed to be lifted and stored for the following year. After a period of great popularity during the early nineteenth century, they went slightly out of favour but, like the chrysanthemum, were to remain as a show bloom in allotments and small gardens up and down the country. Their late flowering season and brilliant colour range made dahlias a favourite with gardeners and flower arrangers, and space was often found in even the smallest town garden for a row or two of pom-poms or miniature ball blooms.

wallpaper and as an inspiration for glass, enamelling and paintings in the art nouveau movement. Lilies were most commonly grown in large pots to stand indoors or on terraces and in conservatories. Gertrude Jekyll suggested that they be grown in their natural woodland setting amongst the dappled shade of trees as she did in her own garden. The introduction of the *Lilium auratum* in 1862 from Japan had rekindled an interest in lilies and there was now a choice of types which would grow in acid or alkaline soils.

Sweet peas, *Lathyrus odoratus*, had been grown for centuries for their very powerful fragrance and pretty scrambling growth. Early types had very small flowers compared with modern varieties and only produced one or two blossoms on weak, short stems. In 1870 Henry Eckford, while gardening for a Dr Sankey in Gloucestershire, began experimenting and cross-fertilizing sweet peas. Seeing the commercial possibilities of the venture, he left his employment to set up his own small nursery specializing in the plants. By 1900, at the Bi-centenary Sweet Pea Exhibition held at Crystal Palace, Eckford had raised half of the 264 varieties on show. A pale lavender variety named Lady Eve Balfour was considered the most

RIGHT A lovely colour combination is achieved by standing a pot of pink fuchsias in front of a deep purple clematis. The Victorian and Edwardian passion for exotica and conservatories brought the fuchsia into prominence as a summer bedding and specimen plant. Although still popular, many of the newest varieties have changed to provide the size and shape of bloom the breeders think the public wants. Many people, however, prefer the simpler single blooms, which are more in proportion to the leaves and overall plant size, and these are more like the ones grown 80 years ago.

ABOVE This pale mauvy-pink sweet pea is one of the modern types now most commonly grown. Grow them up a fence or trellis or make a tripod of bushy twigs or bamboo canes to support their scrambling habit. If you cut them regularly through the summer they will go on flowering until the first frosts.

LEFT The delicate frilled flowers of the sweet pea look best arranged in this simple way. Mixed with other flowers they tend to get rather lost, although they do combine well with roses. Sweet peas are one of the most useful annual flowers to grow in your own garden as they make wonderful, though quite short-lived, cut blooms.

•◆•

It was a very common practice at
the beginning of this century to
send flowers and other perishables
by the postal service. Country
dwellers would send small bunches
of wild flowers to city relatives
who might never see primroses or
daffodils growing in the wild.
These days, with so many quick
city link couriers and special postal
services, it still ought to be possible
to send flowers to a friend or
relation. Damp moss makes a
pretty and practical packing and
now we have plastic to help avoid
moisture loss, though sealing
flowers inside a plastic bag may
simply make them sweat and wilt.
We tend to pick up the phone and
order flowers from a shop but this
idea shows far more thought and
care than an impersonal bouquet.

•◆•

The Edwardian greenhouse was a magnificent building combining wood, glass, cast iron and usually much white or green paint. Heating was usually via pipes which ran under floors and beds or at the base of walls. Coal and coke were cheap enough to use quite lavishly, so that tender crops could be grown throughout the year and plants such as these pelargoniums reached something approaching the size they might attain in their natural habitat. This beautiful example of how to grow plants in a greenhouse is at Crathes Castle in Scotland, and it probably looks now as it might have done eighty or so years ago. The tall fern plants have a very old-fashioned feel. At one time these were grown to provide sprays for bouquets, buttonholes and decorations and sometimes to decorate dishes for a cold buffet.

outstanding variety ever raised and was used for the presentation bouquet at the exhibition. It is still possible to buy some of these Eckford named types today from seed suppliers.

At about the same time a chance sweet pea seedling appeared with frilled petals in the garden at Althorp Park, the Northamptonshire home of the Countess Spencer. The gardener, Silas Cole, spotted the flower and named it after the Countess and in the following year there appeared another version of this flower in the Cambridgeshire garden of a Mr W J Unwin. Unwin was a grocer who grew sweet peas as a hobby but once he realized that his form would breed true, he sold his business and began growing sweet peas for the thriving cut-flower industry, producing many new varieties. The sweet pea quickly became a popular flower to grow for exhibition. It did not take up too much space and no elaborate equipment or artificial heat was needed. It captured the imagination of the public and has remained one of the best loved and most commonly grown hardy annuals.

The great plant hunters at this time were still risking life and limb to bring back novel plants. E H Wilson, who was contracted by the Veitch nursery to collect for them, visited western China, Japan, Formosa and Korea, and during his plant hunting days is credited as having introduced over a thousand new plants. A sample from the list of those he discovered reads: *Davidia involucrata* or the handkerchief tree, 56 species of rhododendron, *Clematis armandii, Kolkwitzia amabilis, Magnolia delavayi,* and *Lilium regale* which caused him a broken leg. There were numerous primula species and nine acers. Following on from Wilson, George Forrest is believed to have discovered 309 new species and introduced 335 species altogether. He concentrated on rhododendrons but also introduced many of the wonderful and showy Asiatic primulas which are still immensely popular.

Francis Kingdon-Ward was another plant collector who worked during this period. He visited Szechwan and Yunnan in China and also much of Asia, and his name is associated with lilies, gentians and primulas. In 1925 he collected the giant cowslip *Primula florindae* in Tibet and in the same year the famous blue poppy *Meconopsis betonicifolia* which, with its extraordinary colour and fussiness of conditions, made it an instant star in the plant theatre.

More humdrum and everyday flowers which were loved at this time included the pelargoniums – all the scented leaf varieties and the regals. Whether they were sprawling in a cottage window or cosseted in a glasshouse, they were universally popular. Gertrude Jekyll describes one of the scented leaf varieties, *Pelargonium tomentosum,* as being 'thick as a fairy's blanket . . . and to be found in most old-fashioned gardens'. She used the leaves to make peppermint jelly and they were also used to scent or flavour food or float in fingerbowls of water. There are pelargoniums with eucalyptus scent, orange and lemon scent, peppermint and balsam scent as well as subtle perfumes almost impossible to describe. Lady Mary, a prettily flowered variety popular at this time, has what is described as a nutmeg scent while Purple Unique possesses the scent of absinthe. Leaves were plucked to put with a flower for a buttonhole or tucked into a pocket or prayerbook on the way to church to be fingered and so release the scent in a stuffy or musty room.

Other popular cottage garden flowers were asters and lupins, dahlias and michaelmas daisies and, for a porch or window, fuchsias were grown in pots or hanging baskets to add a touch of the exotic to simple surroundings.

RIGHT The blue Himalayan poppy caused a sensation when it was first discovered and brought to England by Frank Kingdon-Ward. It demands moist peaty soil and shady light-woodland conditions to thrive. It is a challenging plant to grow but gardeners try hard with it, dreaming of swathes of azure blue.

Edwardian Floral Decoration

B y Edwardian times people were tired to some extent of the over elaborate and fussy flower arrangements and table decorations favoured in the previous century. Queen Alexandra, while still Princess of Wales, was supposed to have decorated the drawing room of Marlborough House with 'common' beech boughs, which probably looked superb but were unusual enough to cause surprised comment. There was a hint of Japanese influence in the air and the first Japanese-style gardens were being laid out in Britain by a few brave nonconformist gardeners. There was a craving for freshness and simplicty and a desire to use plant material in a natural and uncontrived way. One famous book on flower arranging, published in 1906, had many ideas for cut-flower arrangements done in a new way,

RIGHT Home-made lemonade and a light and airy old-fashioned sponge cake set the scene for an afternoon of tennis or just sitting in the shade on a summer day. The flowers help to evoke an Edwardian herbaceous border in a mix of pinks, reds and white. An old enamel water jug makes the perfect container for an armful of long-stemmed flowers picked from the garden. There are tall white larkspur and astilbe in various shades. The prickly hooded flowers of acanthus contrast with the trumpet flowers of annual mallow. The purple spikes are veronica and in the foreground there are shorter stems of pinks and pelargoniums.

LEFT The perennial form of the lupin was introduced into Britain from Virginia in 1637 by John Tradescant and was grown in gardens in its well-known purplish-blue form until George Russell of York produced his strain of Russell lupins in 1937. Amongst the lupins growing here in a colour scheme of white, mauve and pink are sweet rocket plants sometimes known as dame's violet or damask violet (*Hesperis matronalis*). These simple cottage garden plants are easy to grow and the white or mauve flowers possess the most delicious perfume which carries particularly on the night air.

RIGHT The decoration for a hat need not be crumpled artificial flowers and tired ribbon, but instead a great mass of fresh roses. The Edwardians loved hats of all kinds, particularly large ones weighed down with decoration. For an occasion such as a wedding, a hat only needs to look its best for a few hours, so it is possible to use fresh flowers. Choose roses which have just opened or are only just fully open. Be sure they have been well-conditioned first and cut the stems off quite short. Wrap the ends in florist tape to seal in the cut end and then pin or stitch the flowers round the hat crown.

ABOVE Annual shirley poppies look their best covering a large area of ground. They are not as pretty crammed in amongst other plants, as they need light and space around them to best show off the translucency of their petals and their range of brilliant colours. Seed sown in autumn will produce the earliest blooms the following year from late May to July. A spring sowing of seed will result in flowers from July onwards.

RIGHT This small greenhouse is full of different varieties of pelargoniums – many scented-leaf types as well as the regal pelargoniums, zonal pelargoniums and some smaller miniature regals. They still thrive in gritty soil and seem happiest in clay pots rather than plastic ones. Some varieties will flower on and off right through the year but most put on their best display in late spring and early summer. The greenhouse must be kept free of frost during the winter but does not have to be much above freezing for the plants to survive. During the summer they will all enjoy being stood outside or planted into the garden where some will become colossal plants after just a few months.

❦

❦

LEFT By Edwardian times the relatively new fashion for large and elaborate bridal bouquets was at its peak. Here, in the style of the period, is a sumptuous cream sheaf of flowers. It is perfectly possible to make a bouquet of this type yourself and it does not need to be wired as it might be by a professional florist. Begin by taking the longest stems of flowers which make the base of the spray and slowly build onto these, working up the bouquet. You can do this in your hands or lay the flowers down on a flat surface. Every now and again wire the stems at the top to hold the bunch together and continue building up the flowers. Keep the large and important blooms for the front and top of the spray, and use some greenery such as fern to delineate the top edge of the flowers. Amongst the flowers used here are white single-stemmed roses, cream spray roses, bridal gladioli, cream spray carnations, myrtle leaves and flowers (a traditional addition to a bride's bouquet), white lilies and cream sweet peas.

a 'free' style as it was called. The author admitted that he had been influenced by the Japanese way of using flowers. The rise of the flower shop, which provided cut flowers whenever needed, reduced the demands on the garden and gardener to produce the material required for special, or even everyday, occasions. By the 1920s, households run with very few staff would arrange their flowers and want to do it in a simple and speedy way. The grandest houses required fewer winter flowers, expensively grown with heat, because their owners chose to spend the winter months abroad, often in the south of France. The acres of glass needed to supply private houses with flowers all the year round dwindled, the numbers of staff declined and it was no longer considered unacceptable to buy produce rather than grow all your own.

Wedding flowers remained as lush and extravagant as they had been in Victorian times but again there was a relaxation in style. The trend was towards showers of loosely wired flowers for the bride's bouquet, which could afford to be lavish in scale while the fashion was still for a full-length gown with wide sleeves and hair piled up into a large silhouette. Orchids or roses were carried by the bride while ferns made a suitable foliage background. The female wedding guests might try to compete in grandeur with wide-brimmed hats laden with flowers, feathers, stuffed birds even, and a spray of flowers or an elaborate corsage would be pinned to the shoulder or bosom.

The fashion for wearing fresh flowers was universal, whether it was a small bunch of violets pinned to an old straw hat to smarten it up, or the elaborate dress described as having been worn by the actress Lily Langtry when she was presented at Court. The ivory white dress had a long train and both the dress and train were looped with Maréchal Niel tea roses. She also carried a huge bunch of the same roses sent to her by the Prince of Wales. Queen Alexandra had a very public passion for flowers and she adored the scent of violets. One variety of violets grown on a large scale as a cut flower was named Princess of Wales after her, and violets continued to be bought in bunches as gifts, love tokens and decorations for a sash or hat.

The Stylized Flower

T he various art movements at this time took the flower into many areas of the decorative arts where, often stylized, it found its way onto jewellery, fabrics, furniture, ceramics and stained glass. Art nouveau themes were derived almost exclusively from nature, following the curves and sinuous lines of flower stems or birds' plumage. Flowers which appeared time and again were lilies, poppies, irises, roses, and waterlilies with the focus as much on the stems, tendrils, seedheads and buds as on the flowers themselves.

Often the flowers or plants were abstracted almost beyond recognition but were always the starting point for the sensuous lines and curvilinear shapes. Glass became an important material used either flat in stained-glass windows or blown into vases and bowls or the famous Tiffany lamp shades. Some of the simple and narrow glass vases of this period defined, by their strong visual statement, the kinds of flowers that they could contain. Charles Rennie Mackintosh, the architect, was known to decorate his own home with bowls of bare, coloured twigs, a style which suited his spare and graceful interiors but would have been slightly too daring even for the fashionable woman of the day. But there was a general move in this direction and it was only a small step on from jugs of silvery honesty seedheads, a common Edwardian decoration, to the quiet sophistication of subtle winter twigs.

RIGHT Here a collection of several different types of lilies are growing in the semi-woodland position that they generally prefer. As plants they can be quite tricky to place in the garden as they have a definitely exotic style about them and do not mix happily with many other flowers. Often grown in pots which can be moved around and positioned for maximum impact, they are now almost better known as cut flowers which are available all the year round. Few of us would sacrifice any of these blooms for a vase indoors, but once cut they last for an extremely long time in water and they are always strikingly bold in shape and colour.

INDEX
OF PLANT NAMES
—•—